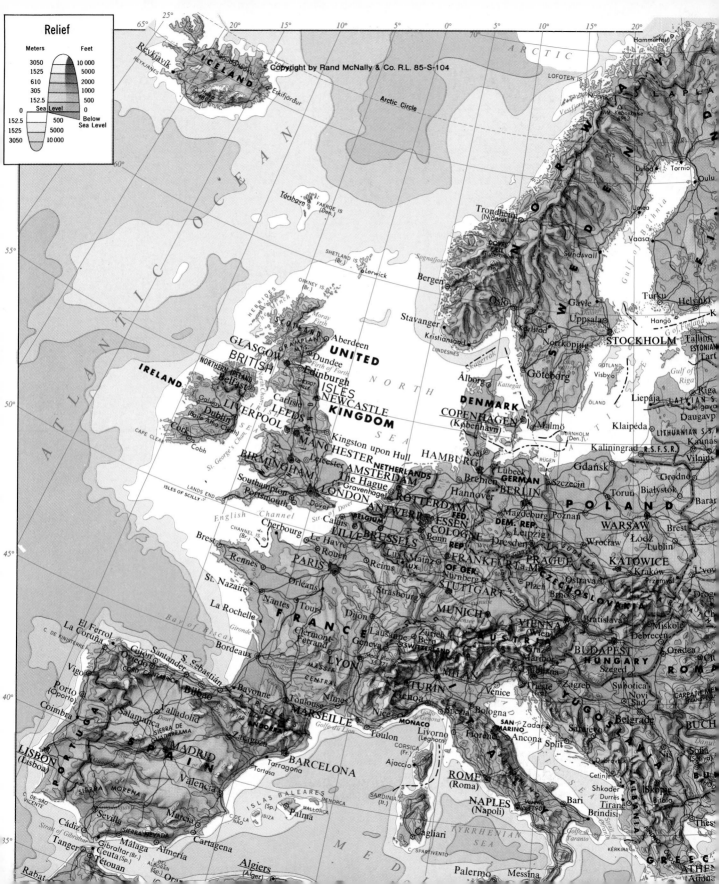

Relief

Meters		Feet
3050		10 000
1525		5000
610		2000
305		1000
152.5		500
0	Sea Level	0
152.5		500
1525	Below Sea Level	5000
3050		10 000

Copyright by Rand McNally & Co. R.L. 85-S-104

ARCTIC OCEAN

Hammerfest

Reykjanes

REYKJAVIK

ICELAND

Eskifjördur

Arctic Circle

LOFOTEN IS.

Narvik

Kebnekaise

LAPLA

NORWAY

SWEDEN

FINLAND

Luleå

Tornio

Oulu

Tórshavn

FAEROE IS. (Den.)

Trondheim (Nidaros)

Umeå

Gulf of Bothnia

SHETLAND IS. (Br.)

Lerwick

Bergen

Sundsvall

Vaasa

Stavanger

Oslo

Gävle

Turku

Helsinki

ORKNEY IS. (Br.)

Moray Firth

Kristiansand

Karlstad

Uppsala

Hangö

Gulf of Finland

Tallinn

ESTONIAN S.S.

Tartu

HEBRIDES

GLASGOW

SCOTLAND

Aberdeen

Norrköping

STOCKHOLM

Göteborg

Visby

GOTLAND

Riga

Gulf of Riga

BRITISH

GRAMPIAN MTS.

Dundee

UNITED

NORTH

Ålborg

Kattegat

ÖLAND

Liepaja

LATVIAN S.S.

Daugavp

IRELAND

NORTHERN IRELAND

Belfast

Edinburgh

Firth of Forth

ISLES

Carlisle

KINGDOM

SEA

DENMARK

COPENHAGEN (København)

Malmö

BORNHOLM (Den.)

Klaipėda

LITHUANIAN S.S.

Kaunas

R.S.F.S.R.

Galway

Dublin Bâile Átha Cliath

LIVERPOOL

LEEDS

NEWCASTLE

Kiel

Lübeck

RÜGEN

Gdansk

Vilnius

Grodno

Cork

Cobh

CAPE CLEAR

St. George's Channel

BIRMINGHAM

Leicester

MANCHESTER

Kingston upon Hull

HAMBURG

Bremen

GERMAN

Szczecin

Torun

Białystok

Barar

LANDS END

Southampton

Portsmouth

LONDON

AMSTERDAM

The Hague 'sGravenhage

NETHERLANDS

Hannover

Magdeburg

BERLIN

FED.

Poznań

POLAND

WARSAW

Brest

ISLES OF SCILLY

English Channel

Str. of Dover Dover

Calais

ANTWERP

ROTTERDAM

BELGIUM

ESSEN

COLOGNE

Bonn

DEM. REP.

Leipzig

Dresden

Wrocław

Łódź

Lublin

CHANNEL IS. (Br.)

Cherbourg

Le Havre

Rouen

LILLE

BRUSSELS

Lux. Mainz

REP.

FRANKFURT

OF GER.

PRAGUE

KATOWICE

L'vov

Przemyśl

Brest

Rennes

Reims

Luxembourg

Nürnberg

La M...

Plzeň

CZECHOSLOVAKIA

Ostrava

Kraków

Drog

PARIS

Strasbourg

STUTTGART

Brno

Orléans

Danube

Drog

St. Nazaire

Tours

Dijon

MUNICH

Bodensee

VIENNA (Wien)

Bratislava

Miskolc

Debrecen

Ch...

Nantes

La Rochelle

FRANCE

Clermont-Ferrand

Lausanne

Zürich

Bern

SWITZERLAND

Graz

Martin

ROMA

C. DE FINISTERRE

El Ferrol

La Coruña

Santiago

Gijón

Oviedo

Santander

S. Sebastián

Bayonne

Geneva

Mont Blanc 15,771

AUSTRIA

BUDAPEST

HUNGARY

Oradea

Cl

Vigo

Porto (Oporto)

Coimbra

PORTUGAL

Bilbao

PYRENEES

Toulouse

LYON

MASSIF CENTRAL

Gironde

MILAN

Trieste

Zagreb

Novi Sad

Subotica

Szeged

CARPATHIE

Salamanca

SIERRA DE GUADARRAMA

Valladolid

Zaragoza

ANDORRA

Nîmes

MARSEILLE

TURIN

Genoa

Venice

Bologna

YUGOSLAVIA

Belgrade

BUCH

LISBON (Lisboa)

SPAIN

MADRID

Tortosa

BARCELONA

Toulon

Golfe du Lion

CORSICA (Fr.)

MONACO

Livorno (Leghorn)

Nice

La Spezia

SAN MARINO

Florence

Ancona

Zadar

Split

Sarajevo

Dubrovnik

Niš

Sofia (Sofiya)

BU

Valencia

SIERRA MORENA

Murcia

ISLAS BALEARES (Sp.)

IBIZA

MALLORCA

Palma

Menorca

SARDINIA (It.)

ROME (Roma)

Zadar

Vesuvius 4190

Bari

Cetinje

Shkodër

Durrës

Tirané

BU

Iskope

ALBANIA

Bitola

C. DE SÃO VICENTE

Cádiz

Sevilla

SIERRA NEVADA

Almería

Cagliari

TYRRHENIAN SEA

NAPLES (Napoli)

Brindisi

C. SPARTIVENTO

Golfo di Taranto

KÉRKIRA

GREECE

Thess

Málaga

Gibraltar (Br.)

Ceuta (Sp.)

DEL ALBORAN

Cartagena

ADRIATIC SEA

Tanger

Tétouan

Algiers (Alger)

Ora...

Palermo

Messina

MED

ATHEN

Amb...

Rabat

© Copyright by Rand McNally & Co. R.L. 86-S-63

Enchantment of the World

FRANCE

By Peter Moss and Thelma Palmer

Consultant: Lawrence M. Sommers, Ph.D., Professor of Geography, Michigan State University, East Lansing, Michigan

Consultant: Christiane Kelley, Alliance Française-Maison Française, Chicago, Illinois

Consultant for Reading: Robert L. Hillerich, Ph.D., Bowling Green State University, Bowling Green, Ohio

CHILDRENS PRESS ®

CHICAGO

Amboise, on the Loire River, was the last home of Italian Renaissance artist Leonardo da Vinci.

Library of Congress Cataloging-in-Publication Data

Moss, Peter.
  France.

  (Enchantment of the world)
  Includes index.
  Summary: An introduction to the history, geography, climate, government, economy, industries, culture, and major cities of France.
  1. France—Juvenile literature. [1. France]
I. Palmer, Thelma. II. Title.
DC17.M67 1986   944   86-9628
ISBN 0-516-02761-1

Picture Acknowledgments
© **Mary Ann Brockman:** 46 (top), 82 (bottom)
© **Cameramann International, Ltd.:** 10 (left), 40, 45, 48 (left), 69, 73 (left), 86 (left), 108 (right), 111 (bottom)
© **Joan Dunlop:** 76 (right), 102
© **Tony Freeman:** 103 (right)
Courtesy French Government Tourist Office: 10 (right), 12, 54 (left), 93 (right), 98, 100 (right)
Gartman Agency: © Michael Philip Manheim—111 (top right); © Diane Schmidt—66, 106 (right)
Historical Pictures Service, Chicago: 15, 17, 24, 71 (2 photos), 74 (2 photos), 76 (left), 81, 104 (bottom)

Image Finders: © Bob Skelly—43 (left)
Journalism Services: © Dirk Gallian—104 (top); © Rene Sheret—86 (right)
© **Greg Laun:** 9 (left), 27
Nawrocki Stock Photo: © Jeff Apoian—8 (left), 52, 89; © Ted Cordingley—111 (top left), 113; © William S. Nawrocki—23, 68; © Robert Perron—46 (bottom), 90 (top); © Mark L. Stevenson—11; © D. J. Variakojis—87
© **Chip and Rosa Maria Peterson:** 101
Chip and Rosa Maria Peterson: © Nancy Guiguere/Bruce Tyler—103 (left)
The Photo Source International: Cover, 8 (right), 84 (left)
© **Photri:** 18 (right), 30, 33 (2 photos), 36, 39 (right), 42 (2 photos), 49 (left), 51 (right), 53 (2 photos), 54 (right), 58 (left), 63 (right), 64 (3 photos), 79 (right), 93 (left), 94, 99, 100 (left), 106 (left), 107 (2 photos)
R/C Photo Agency: © Chevalier—79 (left)
Root Resources: © Jane P. Downton—82 (top); © Russell A. Kriete—43 (right), 44 (right)
© **Bob and Ira Spring:** 6, 41, 84 (right), 108 (left), 110 (bottom right)
© **Lynn M. Stone:** 85
Valan Photos: © T. Joyce—72, 110 (top); © Dennis Roy—2; © Klaus Werner—90 (bottom), 95, 97 (left); © Val and Alan Wilkinson—9 (right), 39 (left), 61
Worldwide Photo Specialty: © Alexander Chabe—1, 18 (left), 21, 34, 44 (left), 45, 49 (right), 51 (left), 58 (right), 62, 73 (right), 88, 97 (right), 110 (bottom left)
Len W. Meents: Maps on pages 37, 45, 95, 98
Courtesy Flag Research Center, Winchester, MA: Flag on back cover
Cover: An overview of Paris

Feeding the birds in Paris's Luxembourg Garden

TABLE OF CONTENTS

One of the Loire Valley's most beautiful châteaus, the Château de Chenonceaux forms a bridge over the Cher River.

Chapter 1

INTRODUCTION

France is one of the most varied and historic countries in the world today. Its people, life-styles, art, dialects, climate, resources, and geography vary widely. There are still some rural areas where people live close to the earth. They tend their fields and care for their animals much as their ancestors did. France also has many large cities where people live in modern ways and are leaders in the world of industry and fashion.

Tourists often visit the ancient stone monuments of Carnac on the northwestern tip of France or the caves at Lascaux with their prehistoric drawings of deer and bison. Other visitors choose the castles, châteaus, or cathedrals with their sky-piercing spires that tell of a people whose dreams and faith pointed them heavenward. In this land of contrast, it is possible to ski and hike high in the snowy Alps, while just a few kilometers away people swim and play on the sunny, subtropical beaches of the French Riviera.

The Moulin Rouge nightclub (left) and the Georges Pompidou Center (right) are two striking landmarks of the bustling city of Paris.

If a tourist's taste is for superb food and wine and sparkling night life, there is no finer city to visit than Paris, the capital of France. Here there are some of the best restaurants and theaters to be found anywhere in the world. In Paris there are also colorful public gardens such as the Tuileries, world-class collections of art such as those at the Louvre museum, and magnificent historic buildings. Notre Dame Cathedral is a classic example of Gothic architecture, while Pompidou Center, new and controversial, is an example of twentieth-century architecture. For the shopper there is every kind of store imaginable, from the most expensive *couturier* to the most inexpensive flea market.

If, however, visitors to France want to see the quiet countryside, they may choose long, leisurely walks into one of the many remote rural or wooded areas. There are 18,640 miles (30,000 kilometers) of footpaths in France that mainly follow old sheep tracks and ancient people-ways. In the carefully tended vineyards of Burgundy, the soil is said to be so valuable that the farmers

In contrast to its fast-paced city life, France offers great expanses of quiet, restful countryside.

wipe it off their boots before leaving the fields. Walking the paths of the green Loire Valley, it is possible to visit the castle at Chinon and see the very room where the teenage Joan of Arc met young Charles VII. A pathway along the southern border of Normandy leads through the countryside where the famous Norman cows are raised. Here farmers make a delicious, though very bad-smelling, cheese called Livarot. Indeed, there are many paths and many stories to be found in France. But wherever walkers go, they are almost certain to be heartily welcomed by the people.

Diversity in dialect shows up mainly along the borders of France. France is sometimes referred to as "the Hexagon" because it is six-sided. Three of these six sides are attached to other European countries, and French people in these border areas have adopted some of the characteristics of the people in adjoining countries. This is partly because wars have moved borders and people back and forth over the years. Also, ideas, customs, and languages always tend to mix at the borders of countries.

*Many ethnic and cultural groups make up the diverse country of France,
such as these shepherds of the Basque region (left) and women of
Normandy in traditional garb (right).*

About 100,000 French people called Basques live high in the
Pyrenees mountains on the border between France and Spain.
They are of unknown origin and speak a very old language totally
unlike French. In Alsace-Lorraine in northeastern France, the
people speak a dialect mixed with German. Here, too, beer
replaces wine as the favorite beverage. In Provence in southern
France, people speak the Provençal dialect, which shows the
ancient Roman influence. In Brittany many people speak Breton, a
dialect closely related to that of southwest England. Most people
who speak dialects also speak French as well.

Enriched by these great diversities and contrasts, France is a
strong and unified country. There are probably three factors that
bind it together more than anything else: the dominating capital
city of Paris, a common cultural heritage, and the French
language. French people everywhere are proud of Paris and its
rich history, its leading role in the establishment of democracy, its
outstanding accomplishments in the arts and sciences. Paris,

Called the "City of Light," Paris offers monuments, palaces, office buildings, and boulevards to its residents and visitors.

called the "City of Light," is a sophisticated world cultural center.

The French are equally proud and protective of their language. Since 1635 official French has been guarded by the *Académie Française* (French Academy). This group of forty appointed scholars, writers, and intellectuals attempts to keep the language pure and sets standards of good usage. As a result, French is very precise and clear. The Academy does not want words from other languages brought into French, although with so many foreigners living in and visiting France, this is becoming more and more common.

French was once the court language in England and Russia, and today it is spoken so widely that it ranks close to English as an international language. French is not only practical but also very beautiful. It is harmonious, flowing, and charming to hear. No wonder, then, that this precise and seductive language helps to unify the engaging, modern country called France.

Vivid underground cave paintings throughout France's Dordogne region are more than 20,000 years old.

Chapter 2
HISTORY AND
GOVERNMENT

All through history France has been invaded by different tribes and nations. Time and time again its people have been defeated and their villages and towns destroyed. But each time, France has risen again, stronger than ever.

The first known inhabitants of France were people called Neanderthals, who were short and heavily built. Neanderthals walked erect and had strong jaws and sloping foreheads. They wandered through the forest hunting and living simply. Their tools and weapons were made from stones and bones, and in coldest weather it is believed they lived at the mouths of caves where they kept fires going to frighten away wild animals.

About thirty thousand years ago a race of very intelligent people appeared in France. They are called Cro-Magnons, named after the cave in central France where their skeletons were first found. They had learned how to make fire, and wore clothes of animal pelts and perhaps even a rough kind of cloth. They had no metals at all but made fine tools, weapons, ornaments, needles, and combs from ivory, bone, or stone. But the most remarkable things these people left are the beautiful paintings on the walls of some of the caves.

THE CELTS AND THE ROMANS

Little is known of France during the many thousands of years after the Cro-Magnons lived there. Then, about 1000 B.C., tribes of people called Celts moved into the rich lands on the western edge of the continent from central Europe. The Celts were much better organized than the earlier peoples and had iron weapons and wheels. They divided the land up into little kingdoms that were always fighting one another. They built small towns of rough wood-and-thatch houses on the tops of hills, putting ditches and stockades all around for safety. These people were among the first farmers in Europe. They plowed little square fields with hand plows and learned how to tame oxen and sheep. The men still spent much of their time, when they were not fighting one another, hunting in the forests that covered most of the land. One of the most important of these Celtic tribes was the Gallia, and all of what is now called France became known as Gaul.

The next people to invade France, or Gaul, were the Romans. In 52 B.C. Julius Caesar defeated the last Gallic leader, Vercingetorix, and Gaul became a Roman province for the next 450 years.

The Romans built great stone cities with temples, baths, theaters, arenas, shops, and houses. Huge stone aqueducts brought water to the cities from springs miles away. Great stone roads with strong stone bridges cut across the country. The Roman law courts and the army made sure there was no more fighting. Life in Roman Gaul was rich and civilized.

The Gallic leader Vercingetorix surrendered to Julius Caesar in 52 B.C.; thus Gaul (now France) became a Roman province.

But the Roman Empire collapsed about A.D. 400 and new tribes from eastern Europe moved in. One of the strongest of these was the Franks, whose name gave us the modern name for France.

The next four centuries are often called the Dark Ages. The new tribes that came into Europe lived in small, scattered villages in the forest. Few of them could read or write. They did not enjoy peace but loved fighting. The Roman buildings fell down and the roads were overgrown with weeds.

THE FRANKS AND THE VIKINGS

Early Frankish kings were known as Merovingians, and the most famous was Clovis, the first Christian king of France. At his death in 511 his kingdom had grown larger, and in accordance with Frankish laws his land was divided equally among his three sons. This custom still exists in France; farms and estates become smaller and smaller as each owner dies.

The Frankish kings went on fighting to add more land to their empire, but soon there were new invaders. Followers of the prophet Muhammad, who died in 632, carried the new religion of Islam through North Africa. They crossed into Spain and then into France. There seemed to be no way of stopping these fierce Arab warriors. Then in 732 they faced the Frankish army under King Charles Martel south of Tours in west central France. The Arabs were completely beaten and retreated. This probably stopped Europe from becoming an Islamic continent instead of a Christian one.

The most famous of all the Frankish kings was Charlemagne (768-814), a member of the line of kings called the Carolingians. He ruled over the biggest empire since that of the Romans, and in 800 the pope crowned him emperor. Under Charlemagne the Carolingian empire was strengthened and new laws were written.

When Charlemagne died in 814, his empire was soon divided among his three grandsons. The eastern part, now largely modern Germany, went to Louis; the western part, now largely modern France, went to Charles; and the middle part—now largely Holland, Belgium, Alsace-Lorraine, and northern Italy—went to Lothair. This division, made 1,200 years ago, has been the cause of wars in Europe ever since.

The next invaders of France were the Vikings, who came from what is now Norway, Sweden, and Denmark. For many years the Vikings had been roaming the seas as pirates and raiders. Now in the tenth century they decided to settle in warmer countries. Some of the Vikings, who were also known as Norsemen or Northmen, sailed up the Seine River and besieged Paris. The king of France was forced to give the Viking leader, Rollo, some land in northwestern France. This was and still is called Normandy.

The Vikings, or Norsemen, sailed up the Seine River and invaded Paris.

In 1066 Rollo's grandson William the Conqueror, Duke of Normandy, invaded England with his knights and beat the Saxon king, Harold, at the Battle of Hastings. William then became King of England as well as Duke of Normandy. His English sons and grandsons also could claim parts of France, so that by the twelfth century the English ruled most of the western half of France.

WAR OF THE HUNDRED YEARS

The French kings naturally did not like this, and in 1337 war broke out between France and England. Called the Hundred Years' War, it actually went on for 116 years and was a series of battles that were often years apart. Armies of both sides roamed up and down France, killing, looting, burning, and destroying. Tens of thousands of heavily armored French knights were slaughtered by English bowmen, whose arrows went straight through the armor.

Above: Joan of Arc, "Maid of Orleans"
Right: Martin Luther, instigator
of the Protestant Reformation

Then in 1347 a terrible plague called the Black Death struck Europe. In two years one-third of all the people and animals in Europe died. During this period the war stopped, but as soon as the impact of the disease lessened, the fighting started again.

By 1429, it seemed as if the English would conquer the whole country. Then a young village girl, Joan of Arc, said that she had heard voices from God telling her to lead the French soldiers and to drive out the English. Amazingly, the French prince gave her armor, weapons, and a horse, and she won battle after battle. Then in 1430 she was captured, sold to the English, and tried by a church court for being a witch. She was found guilty and was burned at the stake at Rouen in northern France in 1431. But though Joan herself was dead, her spirit was not. The French armies, believing that God was on their side, drove the English out of all France, except for the port of Calais in the extreme north.

France now began to make itself into a single nation. The French kings first had to break the power of the great nobles who ruled their lands as though they themselves were kings. Francis I (reigned 1515-47) was determined to make France the most important country in Europe. He built great palaces in the Renaissance style, broke the power of many of the nobles, and sent explorers such as Jacques Cartier to the New World.

THE REFORMATION

After Francis I died, the country fell into fifty years of bitter civil wars over political and religious issues. In Germany Martin Luther (1483-1546), a university-educated monk, disagreed with the Roman Catholic church about many things. Luther believed that the way to heaven was through complete faith in God and not through sacraments and "good works," as the church taught. He also found fault with the church's selling of indulgences, or cancellations of punishment after death. In 1517 he nailed a paper to the castle church door at Wittenberg, Germany, explaining his ideas.

Luther's ideas quickly spread and his rebellion came to be known as the Protestant Reformation. Luther was expelled from the church and called to the city of Worms to go before the Diet, or general assembly, of the Holy Roman Empire. Here Luther defended himself very well; many members agreed with him.

Now other great Protestant leaders sprang up in Europe. One of the best known was Jean Calvin (1509-64), who was born in France and educated at the University of Paris. He became a Protestant in 1533 and moved to Geneva because Protestants were being persecuted in France. Calvin taught that God decided before people were born who should and should not be saved. This doctrine, called predestination, was very different from Luther's idea that men were able to gain salvation through faith.

As Protestantism spread in France, Calvinist Protestants became the strongest and were known in France as Huguenots. Years of struggle between the Huguenots and Catholics came to a climax on St. Bartholomew's Day, August 24, 1572. On that day thousands of Protestants were murdered by Catholic officials as mobs cheered them on. Still the struggle continued, until Huguenot leader Henry of Navarre became King Henry IV. He finally became a Catholic to put an end to the fighting, saying "Paris is worth a Mass." At last peace was restored to France.

By the Edict of Nantes, 1598, Henry allowed everyone religious freedom. When this law was changed nearly a hundred years later and all French people were required to be Catholic, many Huguenots fled to The Netherlands, Britain, and America.

REIGN OF THE SUN KING

Henry IV was determined to make Paris the finest city in Europe. He ordered great squares, roads, and bridges to be built in the capital. His Pont Neuf (New Bridge) is still in use almost four hundred years later.

Henry's grandson, Louis XIV, became king in 1643. He was known as the Sun King or the Grand Monarch. Louis decided that France would be the greatest nation in Europe. He built the largest palace in the world at Versailles, and France became the center for art, architecture, fashion, theater, and ideas. To break the power of the great nobles of France, Louis brought five thousand of them to live in the palace and another five thousand to live in a village nearby so that they could not stir up trouble in their own areas.

Louis XIV, the Sun King

Life at Versailles was an endless round of pleasures: balls, theater, hunting, picnics, music, banquets, and other amusements. Some of the nobles found this life boring and wanted to do something useful—to help run the country, for example. But Louis would not allow anyone to have any part in the government unless he had chosen them to do so.

Louis XIV grew more and more powerful. He started new industries. He made the navy and army stronger than ever. He set up trading posts in India and in North America. He fought the armies of all the countries around him and defeated them. But all of these successes cost a lot of money, and supporting all the nobles was expensive. As a result, the people were taxed more heavily than ever. "The people" meant the ordinary peasants and working people, for the nobles and the church officials did not pay taxes. Indeed, the ordinary people had to pay taxes to the nobles and the church, as well as to the king.

The people of France were divided into three classes, or estates. The First Estate was the church and the Second Estate was the nobles. Together, they formed about 3 percent of the population. The rest of the people were the Third Estate. Most of them were peasants, who were little better than slaves of the nobles on whose lands they lived. There was in the Third Estate, however, a growing class of people called the bourgeoisie. They were merchants, lawyers, doctors, and other professional people. France had a kind of parliament called the Estates General, but it had not met since 1614. When it did meet, the Third Estate had no power.

A CENTURY OF WARS

At the beginning of the eighteenth century, France was at the peak of its power; it seemed almost undefeatable. Then came another series of wars that lasted almost a hundred years. Most of Europe took part, first on one side and then the other; but always France and England were enemies.

In King William's War (1689-97), France was defeated and forced to give up some of its land in Spain and The Netherlands. Queen Anne's War (1702-13) was a worse blow; France had to hand over Newfoundland, Nova Scotia, and Gibraltar to England. Later France lost King George's War (1744-48) and then came into head-on conflict with England in the French and Indian Wars in North America (1756-63). France was defeated in India, North America, and Europe.

The one war in which France was on the winning side was the American Revolution (1776-83). Some French soldiers fought with the colonists but, more importantly, the French navy kept the British from bringing in supplies.

Louis XVI and his wife, Marie Antoinette

By the 1780s the French people were very unhappy. The peasants were not much better than slaves. They paid taxes to the king, the nobles, and the church. They did forced labor on the roads. The bourgeoisie, who were heavily taxed, were very bitter that they had no share in running the country. They read books by the French philosophers Voltaire and Rousseau and the Scottish philosopher Adam Smith. These books said that everyone should have freedom. The French knew that in England it was the parliament that ruled, not the king. Many Frenchmen, too, had fought in America's revolutionary war, which had been inspired by the French philosophers. They had helped other people to defeat their hated rulers and to govern themselves.

The king, Louis XVI, was weak and easily influenced. His wife, Marie Antoinette, and the whole court of nobles spent money faster and faster. The country was almost bankrupt, but the king refused to tax the wealthy nobles or to cut down on spending.

Destruction of the Bastille by Paris mobs on July 14, 1789

REVOLUTION AND INDEPENDENCE

By 1789 the situation was explosive. Two bad harvests had left the peasants starving. War was threatening again, and at last Louis was forced to call the Estates General to try to get yet more taxes from the Third Estate. But the representatives of the Third Estate were very angry. They declared themselves a National Assembly and demanded that Louis grant them equal voting rights and draw up a constitution that would reduce his power. Louis refused, and the mobs of Paris stormed the huge royal fortress-prison, the Bastille. With the help of some of the king's soldiers, they captured it on July 14, 1789. This was the end of the *ancien régime,* or the old way of life. Ever since, the French have celebrated July 14 as their national independence day.

The new National Assembly issued a declaration of rights, modeled on the Virginia Bill of Rights. It proclaimed "liberty, equality, and fraternity" for all and took away the special privileges of the church and nobles. Most members wanted to keep the king but take away all of his power. But after 1791 there was a big change. More and more people wanted to do away with the kings altogether and to make France a republic.

Louis XVI and his family tried to escape from France. With Marie Antoinette disguised as a Russian noblewoman and the king as her servant, the family left Paris at night in a coach. But they were recognized at Varennes, on the Belgian frontier, by a soldier who had seen Louis's picture on paper money. They were brought back to Paris as prisoners.

After adopting a new constitution, the National Assembly disbanded and held an election for the new Legislative Assembly. The members included a group of people who wanted to keep the king; another group called the Jacobins who wanted a republican form of government; and the Girondists, who were moderates between the two extremes. The Girondists were afraid the king and queen were planning to get other European monarchs to invade France in order to put down the Revolution and restore the monarchy to power. To prevent this, the Girondists declared war on Austria and Prussia in 1792, hoping a quick victory would help the Revolution.

THE REIGN OF TERROR

After the death of the royal family, the mobs in Paris and other big cities went wild. Tens of thousands of nobles, priests, and ordinary people were beheaded.

But by 1794 even the bloodthirsty mobs were sickened by killing. All of the original leaders of the Reign of Terror, such as Danton and Robespierre, had been executed in the struggle for power. A group of more moderate men, called the Directory, took over, but the slogan of the Revolution stayed the same: "liberty, equality, and fraternity."

NAPOLEON, SUCCESS AND DEFEAT

Other European countries had interfered in French affairs since 1791 because they were afraid of revolution in their own lands. Now they attacked the new French Republic and, to their surprise, they were thrown back. The French soldiers were now fighting for themselves rather than for nobles. Next the French armies went on the attack. Led by the brilliant young general Napoleon Bonaparte, they captured northern Italy and went on to try to conquer Egypt. But the British fleet under Admiral Horatio Nelson destroyed the French fleet at the Battle of the Nile (1798), and Napoleon hurried back to France. He was elected First Consul of the Directory, which made him, in effect, dictator of France.

The wars ended in 1802, but began again the next year. In 1804 Napoleon disbanded the Directory and made himself emperor. Only twelve years after the French had said they would have no more kings, they had one more powerful than ever: an emperor.

From 1804 to 1812 Napoleon's armies were successful everywhere. By 1812 the whole of Europe, except Portugal and Britain, had been conquered or made allies. Only at sea did Napoleon fail. At the Battle of Trafalgar in 1805 the French fleet was completely defeated by Admiral Nelson, who was killed in the battle.

Napoleon Bonaparte, Emperor of the French, on the battlefield

In 1812 Napoleon made his greatest mistake. He invaded Russia with the Grande Armée (Grand Army) of 600,000 men. Until then Russia had been a friend of France. As the French army marched into Russia, the Russians did not fight. Instead they destroyed all the food and buildings that lay in Napoleon's path as he moved farther on into their country. That winter was one of the coldest Europe had ever known, and Napoleon's army was half-starved and half-frozen when they finally reached Moscow. But the Russians had destroyed Moscow too, leaving it burning.

There was nothing Napoleon could do but struggle back through the snows to France, 1,500 miles (2,410 kilometers) away. Guerrillas, wolves, cold, disease, and starvation attacked the wretched Grande Armée, and only a few thousand men reached home. It was the greatest defeat in all history up to that time.

Now other nations felt brave and attacked France. Napoleon was defeated and exiled to the island of Elba in the Mediterranean in 1814. Then, while most European nations were disarming, Napoleon escaped, reached France in a small boat, and raised, as if by magic, another army. But at Waterloo in Belgium in 1815, he was finally beaten by the joined armies of The Netherlands, Britain, and Prussia. Napoleon was exiled to the island of St. Helena in the south Atlantic, where he died six years later.

The countries of Europe met at a great Congress in Vienna to decide what was to happen to all the nations that Napoleon had conquered. They decided that all of the kings should be put back on their thrones. This included France, which again had a king.

Most of the nineteeth century was a very disturbed time for France. The country was busy building factories and railroads and taking Indochina in the Far East (now Vietnam, Laos, and Kampuchea) and much of Africa. Then, too, in 1848 the Paris mobs went on the rampage again. They drove out the king, Louis Philippe, and set up the Second Republic. Bonaparte's nephew, Louis Napoleon, was made president. But before long, like his uncle, he made himself emperor. Once more France had a royal ruler, Emperor Napoleon III.

In 1863, when the United States was busy with its Civil War, Napoleon III's troops invaded Mexico and put one of their men on the throne. When the Civil War was over, United States troops forced the French to go back to Europe. Then in 1870, a single state of Germany was created out of many smaller independent states. As a show of strength, Germany invaded France and in a few months besieged Paris. Napoleon III surrendered at Sedan. It was France's most humiliating defeat. The emperor was expelled and the Third Republic was set up.

TWO WORLD WARS

This defeat made Frenchmen very bitter toward the Germans and was one of the main causes of World War I. This war was fought from 1914 to 1918 between France and Germany and their allies. Allies of France during World War I were Britain, Belgium, Italy, Russia (until 1917), and the United States (after 1917). Germany's allies were Austria and Turkey.

Much of the fighting took place in north and northeast France, where thousands of square miles of land and many towns and cities turned into a filthy sea of mud and rubble. In a period of four years 1.5 million Frenchmen died here, twice as many soldiers as the United States has lost in all its wars since 1774.

France did not easily recover from the loss of so many of its best men, nor could it make up for the terrible destruction it suffered. All through the 1920s and the 1930s it struggled on with one weak government after another. Desperately it tried to prepare for the next war with Germany, a war that seemed inevitable. When World War II did come in 1939, the Nazi troops of Germany swept through France in a few weeks.

After France fell to the Germans in the spring of 1940, a young French officer, Charles de Gaulle, escaped to Britain with thousands of French patriots and set up a movement called Free France to carry on the war. The Nazis occupied France and set up a government under the World War I general Marshal Philippe Pétain. In the Far East, the Japanese captured the French colonies of Indochina.

It was a terrible time for France, much as the Hundred Years' War had been. Cities and towns were disrupted by fighting or destroyed by bombing. Tens of thousands of French men, women,

General Charles de Gaulle marches in triumph down the Champs Élysées in celebration of the liberation of Paris from German occupation, August 25, 1944.

and children escaped into the forests and mountains to join the Resistance movement. They blew up railroads and bridges, sabotaged factories and shipyards, and made life difficult for the Germans in France. Many thousands of Resistance fighters, even small children and old people, were executed.

On June 4, 1944, the Allied forces—the United States, Britain, Free France, and many others—stormed ashore for the D-Day invasion of Normandy. It was a long, slow, and costly fight, but at last the war in Europe ended in 1945, with the whole continent broken and starving.

General de Gaulle became president of France, and the Fourth Republic was established. But it was the same old story of many political parties and weak governments. It was only with money and materials from the United States that France stayed alive. In 1946, de Gaulle resigned as president "forever" because French politics were in such a mess.

Then slowly things began to get better. France realized that the world was a much smaller place than it had been in 1939, and the atomic bomb that ended World War II had given war a terrible new meaning. Europe was now divided into two blocks, the communist East and the democratic West. In 1949 France joined with fourteen other Western nations, including the United States and Canada, to form the North Atlantic Treaty Organization (NATO) for Western defense. After a short time West Germany joined too, and France realized that it must learn to live with its old enemy. In seventy-five years the two had fought three savage wars, and there could not be a fourth.

In 1952 France, Belgium, Luxembourg, The Netherlands, and West Germany joined in the European Coal and Steel Community. They agreed to have the same conditions and prices for mining and heavy industry. They eliminated tariffs among themselves on coal and steel products. This was a very important step in breaking down the old rivalry between European countries.

In 1958 they went much further, and together with Italy, they set up the European Economic Community (EEC), or Common Market. The six countries agreed to work toward complete freedom of movement without passports, just as people move freely between states in the United States. They also agreed to work toward having the same taxes and doing away with customs duties.

But while life was improving at home, things were getting worse in the colonies. French troops had tried to take back Indochina after World War II, but at once a guerrilla war began for independence in Vietnam. Led by Ho Chi Minh, the Vietnamese defeated the troops of the Légion Étrangère (Foreign Legion), a tough fighting force made up of the elite of the French army. Created in 1831 to serve outside France, men often joined the Legion to escape political or criminal punishment, but others joined for high adventure. In spite of the toughness of these colorful fighting men, Vietnam became independent in 1954.

In Africa, too, colony after colony became independent, generally without fighting, until only Algeria was left. Algeria was special. It was a major producer of oil, which France badly needed. Also, more than a million French people lived there as farmers and settlers. These colonists wanted Algeria to remain French. Bitter guerrilla war broke out; terrorist bombings, torture, and massacres occurred every day. France itself was divided and seemed on the edge of civil war. Then the army asked General de Gaulle to come back and take over. He agreed, but only if he were given complete power, and so he returned as a virtual dictator. The Fourth Republic was ended and the Fifth began.

Algeria eventually gained independence, and after some struggles France began to pull itself out of despair. The Fifth Republic was very independent and was particularly unhappy about having to depend on the United States for help. It withdrew from NATO and set up its own atomic and space programs.

Yet once again things began to go wrong, and many French people felt their government was not treating them fairly. Inflation soared and prices skyrocketed. People did not think they were getting the social benefits they should have.

In May of 1968 the Paris mobs came out again. This time it was mainly university students and labor union members. There were months of battles with the riot police, burnings of cars and buildings, but fortunately, few deaths. De Gaulle resigned and was succeeded by Georges Pompidou, who was forced to give up some of the power of the president to the National Assembly.

Left: Valéry Giscard d'Estaing.   Right: François Mitterrand

The next president was Valéry Giscard d'Estaing, a right-wing politician. He was an ineffective president, and discontent boiled up in France once again. This time, in the election of 1981, the people voted in left-wing President François Mitterrand. But the people did not like his socialist ideas and laws either, and blocked most of them.

In spite of its great problems, France had made itself into a much stronger industrial nation. Manufacturing and commerce flourished. Exports soared. The roads filled with automobiles and the French homes with television sets, washing machines, and refrigerators. In twenty-five years the amazing French had turned a shattered and starving country into one of the major economic and political powers of the modern world.

The National Assembly in Paris

GOVERNMENT

The government of France today is called the Fifth Republic. It was established to replace the weak Fourth Republic that had come to power after World War II. During the Fourth Republic the president had little power. Most of the power was in the parliament, which voted out the premier and the council of ministers on an average of twice a year.

In 1958 the Fourth Republic was unable to deal with the problem of independence for Algeria, and was on the verge of civil war. It was then that Charles de Gaulle formed a new government that gave the president much more power.

The president of France is elected for a seven-year term by voters who are at least eighteen years old. The parliament consists of the National Assembly and the Senate. The 491 members of the National Assembly are elected by the people for five-year terms. The Senate is less powerful, and its 280 members are chosen for nine-year terms by regional and city officials.

The most powerful man in France now is the president. He chooses the prime minister and other ministers who form the government, or cabinet. He can dismiss the National Assembly and order a new election. He can also hold referendums; that is, if there is a very important matter, he can ask the people to vote on it directly and not leave it to the National Assembly or government. In an exceptional emergency, the president can take almost complete power and rule as a dictator. Many French people are worried about the great powers of the president and would like to see the National Assembly have more power. Although it is unlikely to happen again, the French know from their history what can happen when a powerful ruler such as Louis XIV or Napoleon takes over.

France is divided into ninety-six departments, and each is administered by an elected General Council. The government appoints a kind of governor called a commissioner (formerly called a prefect) who, together with the General Council, runs the affairs of the department. There are also five departments that govern French overseas possessions.

The commune is the basic unit of French government. There are approximately 38,000 communes, which vary in size from small villages to large cities. Each commune elects a council, and the council then elects a mayor from among its members.

Just as Paris, the capital of France, is noted for its beauty and culture, it is also noted for its government. It is both a department and a city. Since 1871 Paris had been governed by prefects just as any other department is. In 1977, however, Paris chose a mayor through its city council and now operates under both forms of government. Politically, Paris dominates the provinces of France, although there have been recent attempts to decentralize.

·Deep gorges cut by the Chassezac River in the Massif Central

Massif Central

Alps

Jura Mts.

Pyrenees

Chapter 3

GEOGRAPHY

France is the largest country in western Europe. Still, it measures only 600 miles (966 kilometers) from north to south and about the same distance from east to west. Yet within those boundaries is a land of contrasts, a land of widely varied topography, climate, and scenery.

THE MASSIF CENTRAL

At the heart of the country is a high, rugged plateau called the Massif Central. This takes up about one-sixth of the area of France and is made of very old, hard volcanic rocks. It rises to about 6,000 feet (1,829 meters), but over many millions of years the weather has worn down all the sharp peaks. It is a wild, and often bare, land of great boulders and steep, rocky hillsides sprinkled with conifers. Through the rocks run hundreds of mountain streams. In late summer they are tiny trickles, but in late spring when the snows are melting they are raging torrents. These streams have cut deep river gorges and sheer-sided chasms.

These gorges and chasms make communication very difficult. A few roads wind up and down the steep mountainsides in sharp hairpin bends or zigzag along the bottoms of the river gorges, crossing and recrossing the water a dozen times every mile. A few railroads cling, as if by magic, to narrow ledges cut in the rock face. Sometimes they clamber across terrifying chasms on bridges that, from a distance, seem as thin as spiders' threads.

Much of the Massif, especially the higher parts, is windswept and desperately poor. There are few towns or villages of any size. Only in the sheltered valleys is there much agriculture or settlement. Here the usual crops of wheat, corn, and vegetables are grown—sometimes in fields no more than thirty yards (twenty-seven meters) square. On the slopes sheep and goats graze. They are raised more for milk and cheese than for wool or meat. There is some lumbering, but the difficulty of getting logs out makes this only a small industry.

Though land in the Massif is poor for crops, it is rich in minerals—coal, iron, copper, lead, tin, bauxite, and rarer metals such as uranium and small amounts of gold. In the valleys a few large industrial cities such as Clermont-Ferrand and Saint-Étienne use coal and iron for industry. Along steep and winding streets there are huge factories making steel, tanks, airplanes, railroad equipment, electrical machinery, cutlery, and tires.

Until recently the tall chimneys of these factories belched black smoke into the mountain winds. Today most of the factories are clean. This is also one of the biggest electricity-producing areas in France. Many of the river gorges high in the mountains have been dammed. Long, deep, narrow artificial lakes have been formed, and water from them rushes through gigantic pipes to power stations in the valleys below.

*Left: The spa town of Vernet-les-Bains. Right: The Ardèche
River cuts a gorge through the Massif Central.*

In these wild mountains there are many hot springs of water,
some of which contain chemicals such as sulfur. These waters are
said to be healthful for drinking or bathing. As a result, small
towns called spas have grown up to cater to people trying to cure
diseases such as rheumatism.

This bleak, hard country is warm in the summer, with average
temperatures of 64-68° Fahrenheit (18-20° Celsius), and subject to
terrible thunderstorms. In winter it is cold, with average
temperatures of 28-32° Fahrenheit (−2-0° Celsius), and deep snow
for many months. Its roads and passes are often blocked from
November to March or later. With all the water from the melting
snows, it is not surprising that many of the main rivers of France
rise in the Massif Central.

The Pyrenees Mountains, near France's border with Spain

There are two smaller areas of the Massif—the Vosges Mountains in the northeast along the German border and the peninsula of Brittany in the west. Both of these are much lower, so that the climate is less severe and there is much more agriculture.

THE YOUNG MOUNTAINS

Another major type of landform in France consists of sharp, jagged peaks of the young mountains that make up the Pyrenees, the Alps, and the Jura mountains. These are generally much higher than the Massif because they have not yet been worn away by time. The Pyrenees, between France and Spain, are a solid wall 8,000 to 10,000 feet (2,438 to 3,048 meters) high. The Alps, between France and Italy and Switzerland, are even higher. Mont Blanc, the highest mountain in western Europe, soars to 15,771

A cog railroad winds through the French Alps near the resort of Chamonix.

feet (4,807 meters). Today the Alps may be crossed via highways and railways that run through many of the lower passes, some running through long, dark tunnels.

The lower slopes of the Alps are covered with forests. Above the forests is scrub, then coarse grass, and then bare rock. The highest parts are snow-covered all year. The Jura, between France and Germany, are much lower. The highest point is only 5,653 feet (1,723 meters) high, but because the Jura are farther north, the summits are snow-covered for eight to nine months a year.

These mountains do not produce much in the way of crops. There is some lumbering on the lower slopes and summer grazing on the grass above. In summer one can still find farmers driving their sheep and cattle up the narrow, rocky trails as the snow melts. They and their families will spend the summer months high up the slopes in tents until the snow returns.

Wild horses (left) roam the swampy Camargue region of the Rhône delta. This flower-covered slope (right) is a typical summer scene in the French Alps region.

Like the Massif, the Alps and Pyrenees have many hydroelectric stations. And then there is the tourist trade. The Alps, especially, have some of the finest and most expensive winter sports centers in the world. From late fall to Easter, millions of skiers flock to the slopes. After dark they crowd into the restaurants, cafés, and discos. Tired and bruised as they may be, they are cheerful and noisy, and they spend a lot of money. In summer the eager skiers move on to the high glaciers, while the flower-covered hillsides fill with hikers.

The rest of France, in a great circle around the Massif Central, is composed of either flat land, gently rolling hills, or broad river valleys. Here one can see many kinds of scenery—long stretches of sand dunes; woods and forests of every kind; and reedy marshes, such as the Camargue of the Rhône delta, where there are still herds of wild horses.

Besides being rich agricultural land, the Loire Valley has hundreds of châteaus. The Château Ussé (left) is said to have inspired the author of the fairy tale Sleeping Beauty. *The Seine Valley is one of France's most productive agricultural regions (right).*

THE PARIS BASIN

France succeeds as an agricultural nation because of its rich and fertile lowland basins—the Rhône, Garonne, Loire, and Seine River valleys. The most favorable of all these basins, in both richness of soil and farmable topography, is the Seine valley, known as the great Paris Basin.

The Paris Basin, in north-central France, has been the dominant area of France for centuries. Historically, it is the heart of the French nation. Covering about one-fifth of the area of France, the Paris Basin is drained by the Seine River and its tributaries the Marne, the Yonne, and the Oise. A busy commercial waterway, the Seine continues west to the important port of Le Havre. At the center of the basin, the Seine divides around an island, the Île de la Cité in Paris. Outward from this center lie fertile plains, grassy meadows, and gently rising plateaus.

43

Left: Pine trees being tapped for turpentine.   Right: Floating logs downriver for milling

To the north, the plains are varied by hills and forests where French monarchs once hunted. Northeast of the Paris Basin, the land becomes more wooded and rugged. Although there is some farming in the valleys and the lower slopes, mining and lumbering are the more prominent industries here.

CLIMATE

The type of climate one experiences in France does not depend on how far north or south one is. One's distance from the sea, the direction of the prevailing winds, and the height of the land are more important.

On the western side of France, warm water currents of the North Atlantic drift over the ocean across thousands of miles of water. Winds off these warm waters keep the land cool in summer and mild in winter. They bring gentle rain all year. Snow rarely falls in this part of France, except in the extreme north, and then it does not last long.

The resort town of Biarritz, on the southwestern coast

In the south, along the Mediterranean coast, summer winds blow northward from Africa. The Mediterranean is not big enough to cool these winds or make them damp. Therefore, the south of France is fairly dry, with hot summers and mild winters. What rain there is usually comes in winter, spring, and fall. Because the climate is so good, many people from all over the world come here during the winter to live or to vacation.

Northeastern France is about 400 miles (644 kilometers) from the Atlantic. Here, in winter, bitter gales sweep across Germany from central Europe and Russia. Snow falls heavily and lies on the higher ground for many months. In spring, however, these same winds heat up very quickly, and summers here are quite hot.

The Massif Central, where the three main kinds of weather meet, is a law unto itself. The climate here varies with the height of the land and even with the direction in which a slope faces. A valley that faces south might be bursting into life in spring, with corn sprouting and peach trees in full blossom, while higher land not far away may still be frozen in the icy grip of winter.

45

Above: A farm near Grenoble in early spring.   Below: The curved reflector of a solar furnace focuses solar energy on a boiler to generate electricity.

Chapter 4

ECONOMY, AGRICULTURE, AND INDUSTRY

The French economy grew rapidly after World War II. Planning commissions drew up guidelines that reduced both unemployment and inflation. Industry expanded, and France increased its exports until, in 1980, it became the world's fifth largest exporter. Though France trades with the Middle East and other parts of the world, its principal commercial contacts are the countries of the European Economic Community, also called the Common Market.

A COMMON ECONOMY

The Common Market was founded in 1957 to help European nations heal the bitterness after World War II and grow economically. At first six countries (France, West Germany, The Netherlands, Belgium, Luxembourg, and Italy) agreed to work together in economic and trade areas. The EEC today has twelve members—the original six plus the United Kingdom, Ireland, Denmark, Greece, Spain, and Portugal.

In 1981 the socialist François Mitterrand was elected president of France. He nationalized many businesses, though most industry was privately owned. Eventually the government owned the Bank of France, the three largest commercial banks, and about thirty insurance companies. The French government also controlled some of the most important industries in France, such as electricity, gas, coal mining, the Renault automobile company, aerospace manufacturing, the tobacco industry, and the manufacture of matches. It had a 51-percent share in the railroads.

Due in part to big government spending, France was soon suffering from high inflation and high unemployment. Another factor in the bad economy was a worldwide recession that had begun in 1975 and greatly increased prices of imported oil. To deal with the sick economy, the government raised the minimum wage, taxed wealthy people more heavily, and increased welfare payments. These changes were expected to be good medicine for what ailed France, but they did not help. The value of the franc reached a new low and had to be devalued in October 1981 and again in June 1982. In July of 1982 a four-month wage-price freeze was enacted, but the situation worsened anyway. In August of 1982 France borrowed twenty-eight billion francs from other countries in order to keep from devaluing the franc again.

In spite of everything Mitterrand could do, the franc had to be devalued once more in March of 1983. It was the third devaluation in twenty-two months of socialist government. Then came a 1-percent income surcharge tax, cutbacks in government spending, and a $285 limit on the amount of money French people could take out of the country.

Tourists in France can buy lace from ladies in traditional bonnets in Brittany (left) or bask along the warm beaches of Cannes (right).

France became a good place for Americans to vacation because a dollar bought almost twice as many francs as it had four years earlier. Hotel rooms, food, taxis, and gift items all cost less, and about 1.5 million Americans visited France in 1983.

Indeed, some things were better for French workers, too. The socialist government gave them a fifth week of vacation and shortened the work week from forty to thirty-nine hours. But unemployment rose to 11 percent by midsummer 1985, and Mitterrand felt there was nothing he could do but continue his program of high taxes, slow government spending, and high interest rates.

FARMS, FLOWERS, AND CHEESE

During the seventeenth and eighteenth centuries many of the French nobility moved from their châteaus in the countryside to what they felt was the more exciting life of Versailles or Paris. Some of the peasants, then, were able to gain control of the land they had farmed for other people for so long. By the time of the French Revolution, half of the farmland was owned by private families. These families often lived on the same farm for hundreds of years, loving and caring for their small patches of land. When parents became too old, children took over and continued to run the farm much as always.

Over the years French farmers came to raise a little bit of everything on their land. They kept sheep, cows, pigs, and poultry, and they worked their farms with horses and hand tools. They often had small orchards of walnuts, apples, plums, or, if they lived where it was warm enough, peaches and citrus fruits. They grew all of their own vegetables and herbs and, if the climate was right, raised a few grapevines to make their own wine. Sometimes there were fields of grain and tobacco and, almost always, small gardens of flowers for their own pleasure or for sale in the cities.

On the Mediterranean coast a little to the east of Marseille, farmers began to grow flowers for a different purpose than enjoyment. Here, even today, large fields of violets, lilies of the valley, carnations, and other flowers are grown to be made into perfume. The brightly colored blossoms are taken to the town of Grasse, which has become a world center for perfume making. Grasse, perched on a rocky hill, is not a very pretty place. But when the wind is right, people can smell its heady perfumes for

Left: Flower oils are purified in a perfumery in Grasse.   Right: Some of the hundreds of cheeses that are produced in France

miles around. After the flowers are put through the small factories at Grasse, they emerge as Chanel No. 5 or other perfumes famous throughout the world.

Before World War II France became known not only for its perfumes, but for its cheeses and wines as well. Brie, Camembert, and Roquefort are the three most famous cheeses of France, but there are hundreds of others, made from the milk of cows, sheep, and goats. Brie was named for the department east of Paris where it was first made, while the other two were named for the villages where they were made. Both Brie and Camembert are mold-ripened and are soft in the center. Roquefort is made of goats' and ewes' milk and is veined with dark blue mold. Because of their distinctive textures and flavors, these cheeses are much desired by cheese-lovers and fine cooks everywhere.

The harvest of Pinot Noir grapes at the Louis Latour vineyard near Dijon

THE WINES OF FRANCE

The wines of France, too, have long been considered to be among the finest in the world. Down through the years French farmers became expert at growing grapevines, which are a very difficult crop. In addition to the usual cultivating, fertilizing, and insect and disease control, the vines need skillful pruning and tying. They demand the right soil at the right slope facing the right direction. They need just the right amount of rain and the right amount of sun, at the right time. And if they do have all of these things, a single late frost or heavy rainstorm can make the whole year's crop unusable for good wine.

Left: Bottles of champagne aging in a cellar in Epernay.   Right: Wine stored in wooden casks in a "cave," or underground cellar, in Alsace

All red wines, and most whites, are made from types of grapes that are not very good to eat. The main wine-growing areas in France are Alsace, the Loire valley, the Bordeaux region, the south coast, the Rhône valley, and Burgundy.

Alsace makes a fine white wine from white grapes, and the Loire makes moderately priced red and white wines. The southern coast west of Marseille is one vast sea of vineyards that produce millions of gallons of everyday wine that may cost as little as a dollar a bottle.

The hot, dry Rhône valley makes powerful wines that are often drunk with strongly flavored food like venison. But the crowning glory of French vineyards are those around Bordeaux and those in Burgundy. Here, it is generally agreed, the finest wines in the

Left: Geese are a common sight on country farms. Some are force-fed a rich corn mixture to make their livers tasty. Right: In some areas, hedgerows divide the land into separate farm plots.

world are made, both red and white. A good wine from a good vineyard in a good year could cost more than $400 a bottle.

South of the Loire River along the Atlantic coast, the grapes are not very good for wine and are made into a brandy called cognac. There is another region of France just east of Paris where the grapes make a poor, sour wine. But by a miracle of nature, combined with human skill, this terrible stuff can be turned into something very valuable. These wines come out of their dark cellars after years of careful tending as bubbly, fizzing champagne.

FARMS LARGE AND SMALL

Another specialty of France is *pâté de foie gras*, a pastelike spread made from the livers of specially fattened geese and ducks. Farmers enlarge the livers of these birds by stuffing food down their necks several times a day for about a month. *Foie gras* is known through the world as a delicacy and is very expensive.

Before World War II, many farmers in western France lived on small farms in what is known as *bocage* countryside. This was a small patchwork of tiny fields of all shapes surrounded by hedges and scattered with trees and woods. In the north, the northeast, and the great Paris Basin, the countryside was called *paysage de campagne,* or open fields. In the middle was a small town or village where the workers lived. All around were fields with no hedges or trees to be seen, mostly rolling land with grain or beets.

Whatever the French farmers raised and wherever they raised it, they took great pride in their land. French farming families were independent, and if their methods were old-fashioned and took a little longer, they did not mind. They had lived on the land for a long time and it had been good to them. For the most part, their way of life and their country satisfied them, and they continued to farm as their parents had before them.

When France negotiated its place in the Common Market, President de Gaulle saw to it that the country got as many agricultural advantages as possible. Germany and Italy were more interested in industry, while the French thought of France as the "breadbasket" of Europe. Agriculture minister Edgard Pisani wanted to see family farms of eight to ten acres (thirty-two to forty hectares) joined to one another in collectives and cooperatives. He wanted to ease these farmers into modernization and keep them on their land. In other European countries after the war, modern farming methods had turned the peasants against the land and many moved out of the countryside to become industrial workers.

By 1962 France was feeding itself with almost no help from the outside world. As the Common Market reduced trade barriers, French farmers began exporting foods they had never exported before. French milk, butter, and grain went to other European countries and sold for the same price in Heidelberg, Germany, as in Paris. French farmers everywhere were thriving because they could sell their products to Common Market countries who were busy producing machines to sell to France. By 1979-80, however, France was also very much an industrial economy. During those years France exported 293,329 million francs worth of industrial products and 120,810 million francs worth of agricultural products.

During the 1960s thousands of large, one-crop farms in the north and northeast enlarged even more and modernized very rapidly. There was a switch to new crops. Throughout the country farmers began growing maize, a sweet corn that is rarely eaten but is used for oil. They also began growing sunflowers for oil. Country farming became a big, high-powered business. Tractors hauled multi-furrowed plows across the land. Combines harvested the grains, and beet and potato diggers moved through the fields. The EEC paid French farmers subsidies to produce crops that were not needed in order to keep the farms occupied.

Changes occurred more slowly on the small family farms than on the big-business farms. The Credit Agricole was set up, and, little by little, farmers who had usually paid for everything in cash began borrowing money to buy land and make improvements on their homes and barns. They joined together with neighboring farmers to buy tractors and other equipment they could not afford to own individually. As the farms modernized, fewer people were required to operate them. The young people often went off to universities or took jobs in industry.

The future seemed bright to the small and medium-sized farmers until other European countries began exporting their products to France. Soon England was selling lamb in Paris for less than the French could sell it, and Italian wine was also coming into the country. This made things very difficult for the small family farmer. The disparity between the tiny peasant farms in some parts of France and the vast, prairie-like farms of the central area grew even greater. As more small, scattered plots were combined into larger fields, it seemed that the picturesque, diversified French farm might not survive.

Because of government programs to help small farmers, there was a great surplus of food in Europe by 1986. The Common Market silos and freezers were filled with tons of extra butter, powdered milk, and grains. This surplus was a great worry, and though in some ways Europe was closer to becoming one big community, it was also faced with new problems.

INDUSTRIES LARGE AND SMALL

The most popular image of France is that of the great, bustling city of Paris, set in a land of quiet farms, forests, and vineyards. In reality, France is an important industrial nation, ranking fifth in the Western world after the United States, Japan, West Germany, and Britain.

There are four main industrial regions in France. Two of these are in the north on the biggest coal and iron field in Europe. The north, around the city of Lille, was once the main cotton manufacturing center of France, though synthetic fibers are now replacing cotton in importance. The area now has large coal mines and an engineering industry. Alsace-Lorraine, in the northeast, produces coal, iron, steel, and heavy machinery. It also has large mines of potash for chemical industries and fertilizers.

Left: A fashion show in Paris, a world center for fashion design
Right: An automobile showroom in Paris

The third large industrial area is around Paris. With no local raw materials, Paris industry concentrates on smaller, lighter, and more expensive goods. In both the inner and the outer city there are many small factories and workshops that make high-quality clothing, jewelry, and other luxury articles.

Fashion is indeed big business in Paris and has come a long way from the days of Louis XIV, with his fancily wigged and ornately dolled-up court. The world looks to Paris for new styles every season, and it is not disappointed. Fashion houses such as Chanel, Dior, and Givenchy produce beautiful clothing of exclusive design.

In the outer zones of Paris, there are thousands of factories making products such as aircraft, electrical and engineering equipment, and food products. French automobiles are known for their fine and unusual design, and the automotive industry produces about four million vehicles a year. As early as 1742, an inventor in Paris had a carriage driven by a gigantic—but impractical—clockwork motor. In 1862 a Frenchman, Beau de Rochas, made the first four-cycle engine, the kind that is used in almost every automobile in the world today.

French engineers of the late nineteenth and early twentieth centuries invented many features of the modern car, such as the clutch, the gearbox, and the transmission shaft. In those early days of motoring, it was almost always French cars and French drivers that set the world speed and endurance records.

French engineers have kept up this tradition of advanced automobile technology, often designing cars that seem very unusual at the time. In the 1930s, for example, the firm of Citröen decided that its cars should have the engine power the front wheels instead of the back ones. Most people thought this was crazy. But today almost every automobile manufacturer in the world produces some front-wheel-drive cars.

The French do not make large luxury cars. The largest are Citröens and Peugeots, which are relatively small and low-powered by American standards, but are designed to roll along at 100 miles (161 kilometers) an hour. At least they could until the maximum speed limit in France was reduced to 75 miles (121 kilometers) per hour.

The fourth main industrial region of France is farther south and stretches from Lyon in the Rhône valley to Saint-Étienne and Clermont-Ferrand in the Massif Central. The eastern parts of this

Steel mill in an industrial region of northeastern France

area manufacture heavy steel goods from the local coal and iron deposits. Clermont-Ferrand specializes in railroad equipment and airplane engines. It also has the Michelin tire factory, one of the largest in the world. Saint-Étienne makes general engineering products and specializes in armaments. Limoges, in the west, manufactures porcelain and fine china.

Lyon was once the largest silk manufacturing town in Europe, but though it still has a very large textile industry, its main output is synthetic materials. Lyon is also a very important center for the manufacture of chemicals and electrical goods. Because it stands in the middle of the fertile Rhône valley, with its orchards and market gardens, and close to the famous vineyards of Burgundy, Lyon has a large food-processing and packing industry.

The goats of France are valuable sources of milk, cheese, meat, leather, and fleece. Goat's milk cheese—soft, white, and spicy— is especially delicious when served warm with salads or pasta.

One interesting feature of industry in France is the way in which some manufacturing appears in the most unexpected places. Often such industries are based on a certain skill developed by one family. Or they may be based on some local product and date back hundreds of years to when it was easier to make things on the spot than to send the raw materials by oxcart along mud roads to a larger center. Although today it might be simpler to send these materials to a city by road or rail, the traditions and skills are local, and the little workshops and factories stand where they may have been for many centuries.

Millau, for example, a small town nestled in the valley of the Tarn River, is devoted entirely to the making of gloves. There are many small cottage factories here, where hundreds of women working in their own homes stitch the leather together. They use the skins from the thousands of sheep and goats that graze on the hills high above the town.

A copper shop in Villedieu

Villedieu is a town whose whole economy is based on making copper goods. Beyond a notice that proudly reads "The Capital of Copper" is the main street, lined with shops selling kettles, cooking pans, ornaments, piping, and specialized equipment, all made of copper. In the narrow streets behind are the little workshops where the goods are produced. The local ores have been largely worked out, but supplies of raw copper are brought in to be manufactured.

Thiers, a small town clinging to a steep hillside between Clermont-Ferrand and Lyon, proclaims itself "The Capital of Cutlery." Here the shops are filled with knives, forks, spoons, daggers, swords, spears, axes, hunting knives, cutting tools, and medical instruments. One shop claims to have more than five hundred kinds of pocket knives, ranging from simple ones with a single blade to monsters with a hundred-plus screwdrivers, corkscrews, files, saws, and other gadgets.

Left: A modern autoroute, or expressway, outside of Paris
Right: The supersonic transport, Concorde, taking off

TRANSPORTATION

Transportation is necessary to conduct all of this business and industry in France. There are more than 34,000 miles (54,718 kilometers) of state-owned railroads throughout the country. All major rail lines go into Paris. Highways and smaller roads crisscross the country and measure more than 400,000 miles (643,700 kilometers). It is also possible to move goods in barges along 5,300 miles (8,530 kilometers) of inland waterway, while passenger and freight ships sail out of France's coastal ports.

Paris has two major international airports. The Charles de Gaulle Airport at Roissy to the northeast of the city is the largest in France, and the airport at Orly, to the south, is the second largest. The French government owns Air France, the national airline, and has also collaborated with Great Britain to produce the supersonic transport, Concorde.

The French masters of the late nineteenth century changed the
course of Western art.   Top: *Paul Cézanne's* Still Life *(1890)*
Above: Pierre-Auguste Renoir's Le Moulin de la Galette *(1876)*
Right: Paul Gauguin's Self Portrait *(1889)*

Chapter 5

EDUCATION, ARTS,
AND SCIENCES

Schooling in France begins early and is quite demanding. Most children go to *écoles maternelles* (nursery schools) or to *classes enfantines* (kindergartens). They may start as young as two years old, even though compulsory elementary education does not begin in France until age six.

French children must go to school from the ages of six to sixteen. At the age of six they go to primary schools. Then when they are eleven years old they go to secondary schools. The Ministry of National Education decides what subjects are to be taught in secondary schools and what teaching methods will be used. French schools do not usually have choirs, clubs, bands, or sports programs of their own. The Secretary of State for Youth and Sports organizes these activities, as well as swimming, games, folk dancing, stamp collecting, movie making, and many others for Wednesday afternoons, when the schools are closed.

Schoolchildren of Normandy on a field trip

To make up for this Wednesday closure, pupils go to school on Saturday mornings. On regular school days, classes usually begin at 9:00 A.M. and continue until 4:30 P.M., with an hour and a half off for lunch and two hours of homework each night. Discipline is strict, and French children have a great respect for their teachers.

At fourteen some students transfer to a special technical school for two years, where they study such subjects as engineering and electrical work. When students are sixteen they may leave school or stay on for one to three years taking courses to prepare them for their chosen work or for national diplomas. Students planning to go to a university will enter one of the *lycées* and work for the national *baccalauréat* examination, which they will take when they are eighteen or older. This is a very difficult and much dreaded examination, and up to 35 percent of the candidates fail it. Passing the "bac" qualifies students for one of the universities.

The degrees granted by the universities are *licenses*, which are similar to the bachelor's degree; *maîtrises*, the master's degree; and *agrégations*, which are comparable to a doctoral degree. The French *agrégation* is one of the most difficult in the world to obtain.

The Sorbonne in Paris is one of the world's largest and most famous universities. In addition to the universities, France has various *grandes écoles*, or schools of higher learning, which include specialized colleges and institutes such as the Institute of Political Studies.

ARTS AND LITERATURE

France has produced some of the finest works of art and literature of all time. These have had a great effect on the writing, thinking, and politics of the rest of the world.

Some of the most exciting examples of ancient art were produced by the Cro-Magnon people, who lived more than thirty thousand years ago in what is now central France. On the walls of their caves these people drew and painted the animals they hunted. The most famous of all French cave art is to be found at Lascaux in southern France, where there are paintings of more than five hundred horses, in addition to many reindeer, bison, and other wild animals. Historians think that the caves with their drawings were used for magic and ancient religious rites.

There is a great gap in time after the cave drawings, when nothing is known of the art of France for thousands of years. Then from about 50 B.C. to A.D. 400, the Romans occupied France and built many beautiful temples and public buildings. With their columns and rounded arches, these structures were typical of classical Greek and Roman architecture.

Charlemagne, also known as Carolus Magnus or Charles the Great, was crowned the first Holy Roman Emperor in 800 by Pope Leo III.

After the fall of the Roman Empire in the late fifth century, there was a long period when the various tribes of France were fighting among themselves, but still managed to produce beautiful jewelry, glassware, and statuary. During this time the people also told stories and sang songs about their lives and times. When Charlemagne became emperor in the eighth century, he wanted to bring back the days of Roman civilization. Carolingian artists began to copy Bibles and prayer books in beautiful handwriting and to illustrate them with small, brilliantly colored pictures.

By the ninth and tenth centuries, the Catholic faith had grown very strong, and many churches were built in a new style of architecture called Romanesque. These churches had thick stone walls, heavy pillars, and sturdy, rounded arches. They almost always had square or octagonal bell towers. There were few windows, and the churches were dark inside. The earliest

Chartres Cathedral, one of the finest examples of French Gothic architecture

churches looked very plain but later buildings were decorated with sculptures that told religious stories.

During the eleventh and twelfth centuries, a new style of architecture called Gothic appeared. Builders were becoming much more skillful and had learned how to make walls thinner and lighter and buildings taller by using buttresses and pointed arches. The outsides were decorated with sculptures of religious figures. Gothic church windows were tall and narrow with a pointed arch. They were often filled with magnificent stained glass. On the top of the steep roofs were slender spires. Inside, the great vaulted ceilings opened high above the worshipers, who must have felt they had truly entered a magical place. Indeed, the whole idea of Gothic architecture was a lightness and a pointing upward as if soaring to heaven. The cathedral of Chartres, famous for its 130 stained glass windows, is one of the finest examples of French Gothic churches.

Along with Gothic architecture came the first French literature with which we are familiar. To entertain themselves, noblemen wrote poems and set them to music. If a nobleman could not write his own poetry, he might hire a troubadour (a professional singer-poet) to live in his castle and write for him. The songs were of knights and fighting, but mostly of romantic love. Sometimes the troubadours wandered from castle to castle entertaining people in order to earn their living.

One of the best-known of the love poems of this period is *The Romance of the Rose*, which tells of the problems of a young man courting his lady. The most famous poem about knights is *The Song of Roland*. It is a very long poem that tells the story of the nobleman Roland, who was killed in the Battle of Roncesvalles.

During the later part of the Middle Ages, many people began to question their faith in the church. Scholars began reading ancient Greek and Roman manuscripts. They began to think about life on earth, as well as life in heaven. A movement called humanism developed. This period of the fifteenth and sixteenth centuries is called the Renaissance, or "rebirth."

Renaissance art depicted not only religious subjects but also ordinary people and everyday things. It first flourished in Italy and slowly spread throughout Europe. Two great French Renaissance artists of the seventeenth century were Claude Lorrain and Nicholas Poussin, who are best known for their paintings of peaceful landscapes and peasant family life.

Renaissance architecture featured the columns and rounded arches of the Greeks and Romans but was not as heavy as Romanesque architecture. Instead of square or octagonal bell towers, it used great domes. During this time architects built for private people, as well as for the church.

Left: François Rabelais.   Right: Michel de Montaigne

Until the Renaissance, most French literature had been religious. It had told of the lives of saints and how to live the good life to prepare for heaven. Now, however, with the Renaissance and humanism, great writers like François Rabelais were writing about ordinary people and about this world instead of the next. In one of Rabelais's tales, the characters are rather extraordinary but they reflect the characteristics of ordinary people. *Gargantua et Pantagruel* is the story of a giant father and his son. It shows how Rabelais delighted in the sense and the nonsense of human beings. It is one of the funniest stories ever written, and people still laugh at it some 450 years later.

The other great humanist of the Renaissance was Michel de Montaigne. His writings are not humorous like those of Rabelais; rather, they are very serious essays. This quiet man retired to the tower of his castle to write essays that questioned the moral and religious teachings of his day. He suggested ideas about freedom that people came to believe in the twentieth century.

The palace and gardens of Versailles near Paris

Toward the end of the Renaissance a new, highly decorated style of architecture called baroque began to flourish. Influenced by the Italians, the baroque style features very ornamental scrolls and patterns both inside and outside the buildings. Louis XIV's palace at Versailles is a departure from the baroque. It is the beginning of classic French-style architecture. Versailles is stunning in size. It was almost a small town in one building and housed five thousand members of Louis's court. There are many acres of clipped hedges and flower gardens with fine pathways and, everywhere, magnificent fountains. Inside, the lavish palace is still somewhat baroque. The walls are covered with portraits and tapestries, and the ceilings are decorated with gilt patterns. One room, called the Hall of Mirrors, is almost completely lined with looking glasses.

Left: Versailles's famous Hall of Mirrors.
Above: Gilles, *by Antoine Watteau,*
who helped decorate Versailles

Two artists who helped to decorate Versailles, Jean-Honoré Fragonard and Antoine Watteau, became famous painters. They painted noblemen and their ladies amusing themselves at picnics in fairy woods. There is nothing unhappy in the paintings—just beautiful aristocrats, passing their days in idle luxury. There is no hint of the fact that the real France was desperate, that the people were beset by starvation and constant wars, misery, and bitterness.

The most important French literary form in the seventeenth century was drama. During the Middle Ages, little dramas had been staged in churches in order to teach Bible stories and good behavior. Now, however, playwrights wrote plays just for entertainment. Since the nobility had almost no work to do, they flocked to see the actors in the newly built theaters.

An artist's sketch of two comic scenes from Molière's Le Bourgeois Gentilhomme (The Bourgeois Gentleman)

One of the best of these playwrights was Jean-Baptiste Molière. His comedies, such as *Tartuffe* and *The Bourgeois Gentleman*, made fun of the growing middle class in France. This pleased the aristocrats, who looked down on these people. While the fancily dressed, powdered, and perfumed court was laughing at Molière's wit, however, the ordinary people of France were being overworked and overtaxed to pay for the noblemen's fun.

Eighteenth-century writers Denis Diderot, Voltaire, and Jean-Jacques Rousseau all believed that, given the chance, people could reason for themselves and govern themselves. Diderot wanted to help people learn by collecting all human knowledge together in one huge work, the *Encyclopédie*. He wrote many of the articles himself and imparted the ideas that everyone had a right to religious freedom and that the French government should do more for the people.

Voltaire was a brilliant French writer who showed the wickedness of the ruling classes through what seemed to be a comical story. In *Candide* the absurd hero at last learns that people can improve their lives if they take matters into their own hands.

Rousseau was writing at the same time as Voltaire. In 1762 he published his essay "The Social Contract." In it he said that "natural man" is happy and good and that it is government and society that make him unhappy and bad. Rousseau's essays helped the people of France to believe in themselves and to begin their struggle for freedom, which ended in the French Revolution.

REVOLUTIONARY ART

The French Revolution turned the whole of life in France upside down. Jacques Louis David's paintings *The Tennis Court Oath* and *The Death of Marat* aroused great feeling for the Revolution, and later he was appointed the official painter of Napoleon's court. As the nobles and the church became weaker and poorer, they no longer could employ all the artists. Painters and sculptors began choosing their own subjects, painting in their own ways, and selling their work at exhibitions. More and more, they painted everyday life and common people and expressed their own feelings.

Eugène Delacroix was most interested in color and imagination, while Jean François Millet painted pictures of peasants at work in the fields. He painted people just as he saw them and did not try to make them beautiful if they were not. The name realism was given to this kind of art.

In the middle of the nineteeth century, Édouard Manet and Claude Monet became interested in shadow and light in their paintings and painted mostly outdoors. Their paintings seemed blurred and vague; outlines were not sharp and clear. They knew

Left: Vincent Van Gogh's Self-Portrait.   *Right: Paul Gauguin's* La Orana Maria

that when we see people and scenes outdoors, we do not see them in sharp detail but get an overall impression. Critics called this kind of painting impressionism, and it became one of the great schools of French art. Pierre-Auguste Renoir and Edgar Degas are two well-known impressionists. Renoir is known for his paintings of Paris crowds, and Degas for his ballet dancers.

Impressionism influenced artists from all over the world. Vincent Van Gogh, a Dutchman, lived in France and expressed his strong emotions in bright color and bold strokes. The American James Whistler put great blocks of color together in a painting. The Frenchman Paul Cézanne painted landscapes in strong, angular patterns. Paul Gauguin, another Frenchman, went to Tahiti and painted simple, primitive people. His work, like that of many artists of the period, is better liked today than it was during his lifetime. Today a painting by a famous impressionist might cost $3.5 million or more.

ROMANTIC LITERATURE

As French painters began this new movement called impressionism, French writers also began a new movement that was called romanticism. Romanticism deals with ordinary people and their feelings, rather than with famous heroes.

Victor Hugo is well known for his novel *The Hunchback of Notre Dame*. This story of the hideous cripple, who lives in the cathedral of Notre Dame in Paris, fills readers with horror as the story unfolds. At the same time, it creates a feeling of compassion for the hunchback and allows the reader to see past his ugliness. In Hugo's *Les Misérables*, readers suffer with the hero when he is tortured in the filthy prison where he has been sent for stealing a loaf of bread to feed his starving family.

George Sand was the greatest French woman novelist of the nineteenth century. Her real name was Amandine-Aurore-Lucile Dudevant. She wrote about the French countryside and the peasants she loved so much. She led quite an adventurous life and is remembered for her love affairs with the poet Alfred de Musset and with the great Polish pianist and composer Frédéric Chopin.

Alexandre Dumas wrote adventure stories that almost every French schoolchild still reads today. *The Three Musketeers* and *The Count of Monte Cristo* are alive with the flash of swords, the clatter of hooves, and the last-minute rescues of beautiful ladies.

Though Hugo, Sand, and Dumas sometimes wrote about sad things, their stories celebrated life and the joy of living. Later French writers such as Gustave Flaubert, Guy de Maupassant, and Émile Zola wrote mostly about the sadness and tragedy of life. They may have been influenced by Honoré de Balzac, who wrote about people who were greedy for money and social position.

Two great names in French poetry at this time were Paul Verlaine and Charles-Pierre Baudelaire. Verlaine was mostly interested in the music or rhythms of poetry, while Baudelaire, who greatly admired the American Edgar Allan Poe, often wrote about the mystery of life and death. Baudelaire and Verlaine, along with the other great romantic writers, helped their readers understand stories and ideas through emotional feelings.

MODERN ART

The end of the nineteenth century and the beginning of the twentieth century in France saw even more experimentation in the arts. Many new styles of art appeared in Paris. Henri de Toulouse-Lautrec is remembered for his paintings of the cafés and nightlife of Paris. Henri Matisse, Maurice de Vlaminck, and André Derain were nicknamed *Les Fauves* (the wild beasts) because they used violent colors and all kinds of shapes and patterns in a single picture. Their style is known as fauvism.

All of this excitement in the art world of Paris attracted even more foreign artists. The Spaniard Pablo Picasso, working with the Frenchman Georges Braque, created a style called cubism. Cubist art shows many points of view on a single flat canvas. For instance, Picasso might show the back and front and profile of a woman's face in the same painting. Cubist pictures did not look like their subjects, but broke them up into patterns.

In 1910 a Russian Jew named Marc Chagall went to Paris, where he painted dreamlike pictures representing Russian folktales and Jewish proverbs. His work seems to lead into the work of surrealists such as Salvador Dalí and René Magritte. Surrealist paintings appear to be dreamlike or unreal but still have

Left: Pablo Picasso's
Portrait of a Woman
Above: Henri de Toulouse-Lautrec's
Quadrille at the Moulin Rouge

a relationship to the real world. For example, in a surrealist painting a dog may have the features of a human being but still look somewhat like a dog.

The history of art and literature in Paris after the French Revolution is amazingly varied and complex. It is as though the freedom gained by the French people burst into hundreds of new ideas that had needed to be expressed for centuries. And though they produced more painting and literature than any other kind of art, sculpture and architecture were also greatly changed.

One sculptor who became very famous was Auguste Rodin (1840-1919). Rodin is best known for his sculptures *Le Baiser* (*The Kiss*) and *Le Penseur* (*The Thinker*). These are not highly polished or highly finished sculptures. They were part of a larger project that was unfinished at his death. It is partly because they seem somewhat unfinished that these pieces leave something to the viewer's imagination, just as impressionist paintings do.

One of the most original architects of the twentieth century is the Frenchman Le Corbusier. Using the newer, stronger building materials that were available, he was able to place the inside walls of his structures where he wanted them, because they didn't have to bear any weight. He and the American Frank Lloyd Wright are considered the most important architects of the last fifty years.

MODERN SCIENCE

Modern science really started during the Renaissance. People began reading the scientific writing of the Greeks and Romans, looking closely at their world, and experimenting. They learned many new things about the world and questioned many medieval superstitions. At first, there was much objection to the new science because the ideas often conflicted with what the church and the people in general believed to be true.

Many French people have been important in modern science and engineering. Among them is Antoine-Laurent Lavoisier (1743-94), known as the father of modern chemistry. He proved that when a substance burns it unites with oxygen and that the process is the same as rusting, only burning is much faster.

In 1898 the great husband-and-wife team of Marie and Pierre Curie discovered the chemical element radium, which has been used to help determine the structure of the atom. Radium was also a big breakthrough in the early treatment of cancer, although better methods are in use today.

Louis Pasteur, who developed the theory that germs cause diseases

The Frenchman André Ampère (1775-1836) did early research in electricity. He founded and named the science of electrodynamics, which is now known as electromagnetism. The unit of measurement of electrical current, the ampere (amp), was named for him.

The work of French chemist Louis Pasteur (1822-95) led to the germ theory of disease and saved millions of lives. Before Pasteur, not even doctors knew that bacteria—tiny organisms so small they cannot be seen by the naked eye—could make people sick. Pasteur came to understand that antiseptics should be used in operating rooms to protect patients from infections, and he invented a vaccine against the dreaded disease rabies. Today almost all of our milk is pasteurized, or heated to kill any bacteria in it. Louis Pasteur's discovery of germs is probably the greatest single advance ever made in modern medicine.

Above: Houses along a quiet street near Chambord
Below: Shutters on a farmhouse window near Chantilly, north of Paris

Chapter 6

LIFE IN A SMALL FRENCH TOWN

In a typical French provincial town the day begins when the first person up opens the shutters and peers outside to the quiet, early morning streets. One by one the households come awake. Soon cars and scooters start up and people can be heard calling "Bonjour m'dame, m'sieur." By eight o'clock there are quite a few people on the streets. Some are already going to work, but most are on their way to the baker's shop for the breakfast bread or the delicious crescent-shaped pastries called croissants. French people like their bread fresh and hot for each meal. Breakfast for many families consists of bread or a croissant dunked in a large cup of *café au lait* (coffee with milk).

SHOPPING

After breakfast, family members go off to jobs, household chores, shopping, or school, which starts at 9:00 A.M. Housewives often fluff comforters and other bedding by giving them a good shake out of the open window and leaving them on the sill to air.

Typical French specialty food shops are the boulangerie
(bakery, left) and the pâtisserie *(pastry shop, right).*

Sixty percent of married French women in the cities go out to
work, either full- or part-time. In smaller country towns,
however, the number is lower, so that soon after the children have
gone to school, housewives start shopping. They may go to
supermarkets, which are much like American stores, but many
shoppers still prefer the small specialty shops. There is the
boucherie, for example, where the butcher has no prepackaged
meat but cuts exactly what the customer asks for. The *pâtisserie*
window is full of the most tempting cakes, fruit pies, and rich,
cream-filled pastries. There is the *charcuterie*, a special kind of deli
with pâtés, terrines, salads, meat pies, and stuffed pigs' feet.
Cheeses are sold at the *crémier*.

Most housewives will first head for the open-sided market hall.
There, since early morning, the regular stalls selling meat, fish,

Many French women purchase a day's worth of food every morning at open-air markets.

dairy products, fruit, vegetables, and flowers have been busy. She will squeeze, sniff, and poke the goods to make sure they are fresh and of good quality; but no one minds, as this is expected. In smaller towns and villages there may not be a daily market, but a weekly one held in the village square. This square, which is usually bordered with trees and used as a parking lot, is cleared on market day to make way for the sellers and their produce.

Farmers come in from the surrounding countryside with their fruit, vegetables, eggs, cheeses, and poultry. Some have little stalls; many just sit on stools with their goods in baskets in front of them. Among them are the professional market traders who travel from village to village on a regular round. They may have foodstuffs, but are more likely to sell clothes, shoes, tools, farm equipment, seeds, household goods, crockery, and sweets.

A kitchen interior in the Basque region (left). The French have been masters of fine cuisine for over four hundred years, producing such artistic dishes as this trout in aspic (right).

In most French homes the noon meal is the main meal of the day, but this is changing slowly. In some families, now, the evening meal is the main one, and the housewife begins to prepare it in the afternoon. There is a lot to do—vegetables to be prepared, sauces to be made, soup to be put on the stove to simmer for hours. When the children come home after five o'clock, there is usually compulsory homework to be done.

EATING

The family evening meal usually starts around eight o'clock. The first course may be homemade soup in winter or a salad in summer. The salad is usually a simple one of tomato or cucumber or lettuce sprinkled with oil and vinegar and herbs. The main

Sipping drinks at an outdoor café is a favorite pastime.

meat or fish course is usually stewed, braised, or cooked in some other way with a sauce. Vegetables are a very important part of the meal, and some families still serve a green salad in the old-fashioned way, as a separate course after the meat. Then follows cheese—soft, creamy Brie or Camembert, a pungent goat cheese, or any of the hundreds of different varieties made in France. The meal ends with a dessert—a pastry from the *pâtisserie* or fruit or, nowadays, perhaps yogurt. Wine is drunk all through the meal and is usually an inexpensive *vin ordinaire* for everyday use.

If the family is staying home for the evening, they may watch TV and have a tiny cup of thick, black coffee with, on special occasions, a small glass of cognac or liqueur. Often, however, they have this after-dinner treat at a nearby café and spend the evening chatting with friends or playing cards or dominoes. The café

This bicyclist will be competing in the Tour de France.

owner does not mind if one drink lasts several hours. Until fairly recently many ordinary French homes were small, with little more than a kitchen, dining room, and bedroom. The café was a kind of public living room for them. Some family members may go to the movies, which are immensely popular in France.

PLAYING

Every village has soccer pitches. Many have swimming pools, even if the pool is nothing more than a fenced-off part of a river or lake. The French are crazy about bicycle racing, and many villages have a simple race track. Here, when there are no races scheduled, children tear around the track, dreaming of becoming national heroes by winning the Tour de France, the great 2,500-mile (4,023-kilometer) race that takes place every year.

Parks and village squares become courts for the popular game of boules, *or* pétanque.

In the south of France, one entertainment that never fails is *pétanque. Pétanque* is a bowling game played with iron balls that are thrown into the air rather than rolled along the ground. In every market square, groups can be seen playing on the rough, pitted surface. All around sit spectators, many only half-watching as they take part in the greatest French entertainment of all—conversation. It may be local gossip, but more likely, it centers around the local football team or politics. Whatever the subject, as the discussion gets more and more excited, the arms wave more and more vigorously. To a foreigner it may seem as though a fight is about to break out. But it is all good natured, and if no decision is reached, then there is something to go on arguing about tomorrow.

As night falls the villagers begin to think about going home. They walk along in small groups; they drive off in their cars; they speed away on their bikes. Soon lights switch on in the darkened houses throughout the town, and one by one shutters close upon the narrow streets.

Above: This geranium-laden balcony is an entrant in Bédarieux's floral balcony competition.   Left: Shops throughout France, like these in Tours, may be housed in centuries-old structures.

Chapter 7

CITIES OF FRANCE

At first glance, a large French city may seem much like other big cities throughout the world. There are busy streets jammed with cars and motorcycles and taxis and buses. There are shopping districts, with everything from giant department stores to exclusive boutiques. There are business quarters, with banks and offices. There are crowds on the sidewalks, dawdling shoppers and sightseers, and scurrying businesspeople.

But a second look will show that the French city is very different. The buildings in the city center are much lower, rarely rising above eight or nine floors. Many of them may have modern shop or office fronts at street level, but above they show signs of age. Some are well over a hundred years old. The back streets are older still. Houses three, four, or even five hundred years old face each other across narrow alleyways. Sometimes these small streets are still cobbled and are only wide enough for a single car.

The main streets may have strips of flower gardens running down the center. There are flowers, too, in the squares and at crossroads. Often these are the bright reds and blues and the white of the French flag. Down both sides of the main avenues, there may be rows of trees planted along the edge of the sidewalk. Because there are many cars and many of the streets are narrow, it is almost always difficult to find parking.

Many of the businesspeople dress quite formally. Merchants, shopkeepers, and office workers usually wear suits and ties if they are men, and dresses and suits if they are women. Jeans are very unusual in the French business world.

One thing the visitor is sure to notice, and perhaps enjoy most, are the cafés. Most streets have two or three, and in the popular squares and boulevards there are as many as a dozen, often side by side. Each café has a large room inside with the usual tables and chairs, but many people prefer to sit at the tables that spill out onto the sidewalk. There is a large canvas awning for shelter from the sun or rain, and planter boxes filled with flowers mark the limits. Customers can sit with a glass of wine or a cup of coffee for as long as they like. They can talk, read the paper, plan their sightseeing route, write postcards home, or, most usual of all, just sit and watch. And by watching the people and the cars going by and listening to bits of conversation, they will probably learn more about France and the French than by hours of following guidebook tours around the city.

STRASBOURG

Strasbourg is the seventh largest French city. Since it has the bad luck to be in that part of France near the German border which was once part of Lothair's kingdom, it has been fought over again and again. In spite of the battles, Strasbourg has kept many

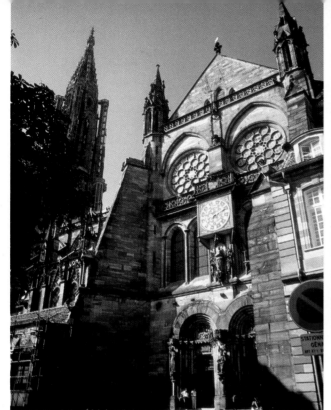

Strasbourg's Notre Dame Cathedral (left) and a street in Strasbourg's old tannery district (right)

of its wonderful old medieval streets, houses, churches, and canals. Perhaps most famous is the Cathedral of Notre Dame, which was started in the eleventh century and finished in the fifteenth. The cathedral, which was damaged in 1870 and then again in World War II, has been restored to its original grandeur.

Another ancient building, the Château des Rohans, was originally the bishop's palace. Today it houses three very fine museums. The district that surrounds the château is called *La Petite France* ("Little France"). It is filled with wonderful old streets with wooden houses, all carefully preserved. A number of picturesque canals cross the area.

Strasbourg is also the birthplace of "*La Marseillaise*," the French national anthem. It was composed on April 24, 1792, during the French Revolution, by Claude-Joseph Rouget de Lisle, a captain of

Strasbourg's Palais de l'Europe, meeting place of the Council of Europe

the engineers. Originally called "The War Song of the Rhine Army," it was renamed because of its popularity with the volunteer units from Marseille.

Strasbourg has some modern buildings, too. One of the best known is the headquarters of the Council of Europe. Here the representatives of twenty-one European nations meet to discuss ways of getting their countries to work together. Many people dream that one day the council could become a kind of parliament for a United States of Europe.

After World War II Strasbourg became an important industrial center. It is famous for its food products, especially the very expensive *pâté de fois gras* (a very rich spread made with fat goose livers). It also makes large amounts of sausages, sauerkraut, and beer, as well as general manufactured goods. Strasbourg is an important tourist center in the Rhine.

View of the harbor in Nice

NICE

Nice is most people's dream city. The fifth largest city in France, Nice sits on the warm Mediterranean at the foot of the Maritime Alps. It is the largest winter resort on the French Riviera, the famous Côte d'Azur. People come here from all over the world to sit among the palm trees, stroll along the Promenade des Anglais or through the public gardens, or lie in the sun all day. In the evening many go to the casino to gamble. Nice is the home of many famous people—film and TV stars, ex-kings and ex-dictators, and millionaire businessmen.

The city is divided into two parts by the Paillon River—the new town to the west and the old town, the harbor, and the commercial district to the east. The old town has narrow, winding streets and is located at the base of a granite hill called Le Château. The castle that used to stand on the hill was destroyed in 1706, but the name remains. The harbor is used for commercial vessels, fishing craft, and pleasure boats. It also offers regular passenger service to Corsica. The most unusual feature of the harbor is the famous Promenade des Anglais, which was created in 1822. It was built by the English colony in Nice as a path along the shore. The Promenade stretches for two and a half miles (four kilometers) along the waterfront. It has two wide carriageways separated by palm trees and flower beds.

Nice is a growing cultural center. A university was established in 1965, with faculties of law, science, and letters. The Musée Jules Cheret des Beaux-Arts and the Musée Massena both contain excellent art collections. In 1966 Marc Chagall donated to Nice a collection of biblical paintings, which are now housed in a memorial to Chagall. Only about a mile from the heart of the city lie the ruins of a Roman amphitheater. Nearby is a seventeenth-century villa that houses an archeological museum and a collection of drawings and paintings by Henri Matisse.

The leading industry of Nice is tourism. Other industries include food processing, olive oil processing, perfume manufacturing, and distilleries. Nice has very good road, rail, and sea transportation, and its airport is one of the best in France.

BORDEAUX

Bordeaux, on the Garonne River, is the eighth largest city in France and the second biggest seaport. It too is very old, with its cathedral dating from 1100 and one church that was built in 900. Bordeaux is known as a modern port and industrial city. But

Left: Nice, a Mediterranean resort city, is full of attractive gardens and parks.   Right: A ship at dock in the port of Bordeaux

above all, it is the great wine city. Right in the center of perhaps the finest vineyards in the world, much of its life revolves around blending, bottling, and shipping wine and brandy.

The leading citizens of Bordeaux have always been merchants and shipbuilders. After World War II, oil refineries and petrochemical industries were established outside the city, greatly increasing the amount of tonnage carried by the tankers that operate out of the port. The port of Bordeaux stretches for eight miles (thirteen kilometers) along the Garonne. It includes five other ports, downstream, that are administered by the city. The port handles both sea and river traffic.

The Garonne separates the city proper from its suburb, La Bastide. Behind the docks that line the shore are large factories, warehouses, and mansions. Then outside the great city squares are the low, white houses of the rest of the population.

The Grand Théâtre in Bordeaux (shown here) served as a model for the Paris Opera building.

Bordeaux is the home of Le Grand Théâtre, one of the finest theaters in France, built in the years 1775-80. Its great double stairway and cupola were later imitated by the architect who designed the Paris Opera. Not far from Le Grand Théâtre is the Esplanade des Quinconces, the largest square in Europe. Among Bordeaux's antiquities are the churches already mentioned, some ancient bell towers, and the ruins of an ancient Roman amphitheater. Some of the gates of the old city wall also remain.

BREST

Brest, in western Brittany, is the seaport city where some of the Americans who fought for France in World War I landed. During World War II it was in a zone restricted to the Germans who used it as a submarine base. The city was almost completely destroyed during World War II and has now been rebuilt.

The harbor of Brest, on the Brittany peninsula

The natural harbor of Brest is well protected from the sea. A magnificent road, the Rade de Brest, extends for fourteen miles (twenty-three kilometers) and leads to open water. The city itself is built on the slopes of two hills. As in many old fishing settlements, the hills of Brest are so steep in some places that people must use stairs to go up and down.

Brest became a major naval base in 1631 under Cardinal de Richelieu. Later the base was improved by Jean-Baptiste Colbert. Colbert initiated the *Inscription Maritime*, which provided for the voluntary induction of Breton fishermen between the ages of eighteen and forty-eight into the Naval Reserve. In exchange for serving in the reserve, the *inscription* offered them and their families security for life. The *inscription* still functions today.

Today the city of more than 150,000 does much importing of wheat, coal, timber, petroleum, iron, steel, fertilizers, and paper pulp. Among its exports are fruit, potatoes, and pyrites.

*Left: Le Havre's Hôtel de Ville. Right: An apartment-lined
city street in Le Havre, leading down to the harbor*

LE HAVRE

Le Havre (The Harbor) is France's second most important
seaport, with a population of over 200,000. It lies on the estuary of
the Seine, 226 kilometers (140 miles) west-northwest of Paris. In
the late 1500s Le Havre was important as a fishing town and sent
boats to the northwestern Atlantic Ocean. As it grew, the harbor
was dredged to accommodate large vessels. During World War I it
was used as a dropping-off place for troops and supplies by Great
Britain and the United States.

Most of the city is built on level ground with the exception of
La Côte, which rises on the north. A tunnel links these two parts.
The Place de l'Hôtel de Ville and the Church of Notre Dame are
possibly the two most important buildings in Le Havre. The
Church of Notre Dame dates from the sixteenth and seventeenth
centuries. The Place de l'Hôtel de Ville is composed of several
great buildings surrounding public gardens.

Mementos of ancient times, Roman ruins sprawl beneath modern structures in Marseille.

The harbor of Le Havre has fourteen basins that accommodate transatlantic steamers as well as freighters and oil tankers. An oil pipeline carries crude oil from Le Havre to Paris. The chief imports include crude oil, cotton, coffee, copper, wool, rum, foreign wines, oil seeds, and dyewoods. Le Havre is also known as a city of industries. Its main manufactured products are rope, timber, wire, machinery, flour, oils, and dyes.

MARSEILLE

The history of Marseille begins with Greek adventurers who founded the city in about 600 B.C. It became a part of France in 1481. During World War I part of the harbor became a British base and many troops passed through. During World War II Marseille was occupied by the Germans beginning in November 1942 and ending with its liberation in August 1944. Today it is a French naval base.

The harbor of Marseille

Marseille is the second largest city in France and is the country's major seaport. It is situated on the Mediterranean Sea 534 miles (859 kilometers) south-southeast of Paris by railway.

The city attracts many tourists. Having the shape of a half-circle, it extends inland from a port called Old Harbor, which is too small for modern ships. Old Harbor is filled with pleasure boats and surrounded by restaurants and cafés. The Canebière is a famous street near Old Harbor that is lined with modern shops.

Marseille's economy is based on trade and manufacturing. The main imports are crude petroleum, grains, carbon, sugar, peanuts, manganese, and many others. The chief manufactured products are bricks, candles, engines, medicines, soap, and tiles.

LYON

Lyon lies in southeastern France and is its third largest city, with a population of over 500,000. It is located at the meeting

Lyon: ruins of a Roman theater (left); an outdoor market (right)

point of the Rhône and Saône rivers, and the commercial and entertainment portion is located on the peninsula between the two rivers. The west bank is the oldest part of the city and contains narrow streets and towering houses. There are twenty-seven bridges connecting thoroughfares throughout the city.

The city of Lyon has its share of historic architecture. The Choristers' House dates from the tenth century and is the site where Saint Anselm, archbishop of Canterbury, composed some of his works. The foundations of the Church of Ainay date back to the fourth century with adopted Roman styles. The Cathedral of Saint Jean is important as an example of transition from Romanesque to Gothic style.

Lyon is perhaps most famous for its textile industry. During the 1500s silk manufacturing became the most important activity. In more recent history, rayon and nylon thread and fabric production were introduced. There are many spinning, weaving, and dyeing plants in Lyon.

Above: An aerial view of Paris, showing some of the many bridges that connect the two sides of the Seine River. Left: The Île de la Cité in 1527, with several connecting bridges

Chapter 8

PARIS, CITY OF LIGHT

Paris, the capital of France, is one of the oldest and most exciting cities of the world. More than two thousand years ago, this great city was founded on a little island in the middle of the Seine River, the Île de la Cité. A Celtic tribe called the Parisii first built their fortress there because it was an easy place to defend and an easy place to cross the river. The first recorded name for the settlement was Lutèce, which means "mid-water dwelling."

By the sixth century the tiny island could not hold all the people who wanted to live there, and the city spilled over to the banks of the Seine. Churches and houses sprang up on both sides of the river. As the town grew, church buildings, universities, and other places of learning and culture were concentrated on the Left (south) Bank (Rive Gauche). Markets, shops, and general community life developed on the Right (north) Bank (Rive Droit).

Typical Paris scenes—sidewalk cafés and open-air markets

Although things have naturally changed and the various
activities are seen today on both sides of the river, the division
that started a thousand years ago is still very apparent. The Left
Bank is still primarily the home of universities and colleges, of
bookshops, and of political and intellectual life. The Right Bank
has the majority of the beautiful public buildings and monuments,
the gardens, the main shopping streets, the stock exchanges, and
the main business offices. Here, too, are most of the theaters, the
opera, and the general entertainments and nightclubs.

Today, metropolitan Paris (Région Parisienne) sprawls outward
from the Île de la Cité for 185 square miles (479 square
kilometers). This magnificent region of almost nine million people
is as varied as the great country of which it is the capital. It is
home to one-sixth of the people of France.

A contrast in moods distinguishes Paris's Right Bank and Left Bank.
Left: Bustling crowds on the Right Bank's Avenue des Champs Élysées
Right: Typical Left Bank bookstall on a shaded walkway along the Seine

The city proper (Ville de Paris) is quite small. It covers only 41 square miles (105 square kilometers), with a population of about two million. Just as in any other modern city, there are streets of small houses and blocks of high-rise apartments. There are parks where children play and older people stroll and sit on benches. There are great factories that produce automobiles, airplanes, food, and fabric. And there is every kind of entertainment, from expensive grand opera to free street concerts.

Seeing the sights of Paris can be easy; ordinary buses run along the streets, and water buses ply the river. But the quickest way, if one wants to avoid the endless traffic jams and honking, is to go by Metro, or subway. Paris has a very good subway system that a foreign visitor can quickly learn to use. There are easy-to-read locator maps, a flat-rate fare, and quiet, rubber-tired trains.

Above: Notre Dame Cathedral
Right: The Eiffel Tower

The Bir Hakim station drops visitors almost at the foot of the best-known building in Paris, the Eiffel Tower. The tower, built of iron framework and rising to a height of 984 feet (300 meters) was erected for the International Exposition of 1889. It has restaurants, souvenir shops, and platforms from which to view the city. From the highest of the three platforms, one can see for fifty miles (eighty kilometers) on a clear day.

The famous Notre Dame Cathedral on the Île de la Cité is just ten minutes by the fast Metro from the Eiffel Tower. This old church, begun more than eight hundred years ago, still thrills visitors with its grandeur—its flying buttresses, its three doors decorated with delicate carving and sculpture, the three rose windows with their original glass, the twin square towers, and the soaring spire. Not as important, perhaps, but certain to catch the eye are the grotesque gargoyle faces on the ends of the rainspouts. (The gargoyles seem to whisper ''gar gar'' when rain spurts out of their mouths.)

Almost everyone loves this great twelfth-century cathedral, but not everyone is as fond of another remarkable building located a few hundred yards to the north. This is the Pompidou Center for the arts and culture, which was opened in Paris in 1978. Made mostly of slabs of concrete, glass, and a network of pipes, it stands out strangely among the older buildings of the district known as Beaubourg. Almost all who visit the center, however, enjoy the many activities such as singing, dancing, and juggling that go on in the busy square outside the building.

The Parisian Arc de Triomphe (Arch of Triumph) is the largest arch in the world and was built to commemorate the victories of Napoleon. It stands at the head of the famous avenue Champs Élysées, which connects with the Place de la Concorde where the terrible French guillotine once stood. The arch is also known as the Arc de Triomphe de l'Étoile because it stands in the center of the *étoile* (star) where twelve avenues meet. An eternal flame burns beneath the arch in honor of the Unknown Soldier of World War I.

Another fascinating part of the city is Montmartre, the highest part of Paris. Some of the winding, narrow streets of the area became five-flight stairways to allow people to walk up and down more easily. Montmartre is filled with shops that sell all sorts of unusual items, from snakes to exotic birds. It is here that the artists, actors, and singers of Paris often make their homes. And here, too, are the lively and inexpensive French discos, the so-called *boîtes de nuit* (night boxes). But the crowning glory of Montmartre is the basilica of Sacré Coeur (Sacred Heart). This gleaming white church seems to stand watch over the city of Paris. To look down on the city from the steps of Sacré Coeur at night is to be caught up in the magic of the "City of Light."

High on a hilltop in northern Paris is the bohemian district of Montmartre, crowned by the basilica of Sacré Coeur (above) and packed with artists' stalls (below, left). Across town, at the head of the Champs Élysées, stands the Arc de Triomphe (below, right).

Above: Indoor and outdoor shopping—an open-air market (left); the Galeries Lafayette, an elegant, multi-tiered department store (right)
Below: The Louvre art museum

And, of course, no one would dream of visiting Paris without seeing the Louvre (Musée du Louvre), one of the greatest art museums in the world. The museum buildings, once palaces for the French kings, now contain 140 exhibition rooms and eight miles (thirteen kilometers) of galleries. Among the most famous treasures in the Louvre are Leonardo da Vinci's painting Mona Lisa, the Greek sculpture Venus de Milo, and the Winged Victory of Samothrace.

Paris is a romantic city of beautiful gardens and parks that invite people to enjoy the beauties of nature, picnic, play games, stroll arm-in-arm, converse, or, sometimes, take a quick nap in summer shade or winter sun. The largest of the many public gardens is the fifty-six acre (twenty-three hectare) Tuileries, which surrounds the Louvre. At one end of the Tuileries are the Jeu de Paume and L'Orangerie. Both were built by Napoleon III, the first being an indoor tennis court and the second a greenhouse.

Today the Jeu de Paume houses the Louvre's collection of impressionist paintings. L'Orangerie is used for temporary exhibits. Other major gardens are the Jardin des Plantes, which contains the museum of natural history, and the Champs de Mars gardens, which surround the Eiffel Tower. Perhaps these gardens are part of the reason Paris has been called a city like a ''woman with flowers in her hair.''

In contrast to the quiet and easy atmosphere of Parisian gardens is the frantic and noisy jumble of Parisian traffic. Tourists are often surprised to discover the speed at which the French people drive and what seems to be a lack of concern for pedestrians and other cars. Horns honk and tempers flare during the traffic jams, which continually clog the streets.

Paris is also a city of high fashion and exclusive shops. The women of Paris are said to be among the best dressed in the world. But if the visitor is more interested in antiques and less expensive items, there are always the marvelous flea markets and the bright flower stalls.

Many visitors to Paris are anxious to try an expensive French restaurant such as Tour d'Argent (Silver Tower). Here the prices may start at about 500 francs ($100) per person. But quite inexpensive, and equally as Parisian, are the excellent small neighborhood bistros and the delightful sidewalk cafés.

Surely, Paris has just about anything the tourist could wish for. Its interesting natives have a taste for the avant-garde in art and ideas but also recognize the value of the past. It is no wonder that Paris, this city of intellectual excitement and romance, has often been called "the Capital of the World." And it is no wonder that thousands of people who visit Paris each year end up at a sidewalk café, under umbrellas or plane trees, sipping drinks and dreaming of the glory that was and still is France.

MINI-FACTS AT A GLANCE

GENERAL INFORMATION

Official Name: France

Capital: Paris

Official Language: French

Other Languages: Persons in some regions speak a local language as well as French. Provençal is spoken in Provence, Briton is heard in Brittany, Flemish is spoken in Flanders, and German dialects are used throughout Alsace and in parts of Lorraine. In the Pyrenees region, certain ethnic groups speak Basque and Catalan.

Government: France is a democratic republic. A president, a prime minister (also called premier), and a parliament form its present government, called the Fifth Republic. France's National Assembly is made up of 491 deputies, elected by voters to five-year terms. The less powerful house of parliament is the 318-member Senate, whose members are elected to nine-year terms. The president serves a seven-year term; there is no limit to the number of times a president can serve. The president appoints the prime minister and the council of ministers (cabinet), which is headed by the prime minister. France is divided into about 38,000 communes, each of which is governed by a mayor and a city council. Citizens over the age of eighteen may vote.

Flag: France's flag, called the "tricolor," is divided into equal red, white, and blue vertical stripes. The three colors were first used as a French emblem on July 17, 1789, during the French Revolution. King Louis came to Paris after the fall of the Bastille wearing a tricolor knot of ribbons on his hat. Red and blue were colors of Paris; white was the color of the royal family. After the royal family was restored to power, it rejected the tricolor. In 1830 the tricolor again became the French national flag.

National Song: *"La Marseillaise"*

National Motto: *Liberté, Egalité, Fraternité* (Liberty, Equality, and Fraternity)

Religion: Seventy-five percent of the people of France are Roman Catholics, 3 percent are Muslims, and about 2 percent are Protestants. About 1 percent of the population are Jews, a higher percentage than in any other European country.

Money: The franc is the standard monetary unit. There are 100 centimes in one franc. Coins come in 1, 5, and 10 centimes, 1/2 franc (ff), 1 ff, 2 ff, 5 ff, and 10 ff. Paper bills or notes come in the denominations of 20, 50, 100, 200, 500, and 1,000 ff. In June 1989 one U.S. dollar was worth about $6.81 francs.

Armed Forces: All male citizens between the ages of eighteen and thirty-five must serve sixteen months of active duty. Approximately 565,000 people are serving in the army, navy, and air force.

Gross National Product (GNP): In 1986, the GNP for France was $724,100,000,000, the total value of goods and services produced by the country in that year.

Weights and Measures: France uses the metric system.

Overseas Possessions: French Guiana, French Polynesia, French Southern and Antarctic Territories, Guadeloupe, Martinique, New Caledonia, Reunion, Saint Pierre and Miquelon.

Population: 55,823,000, including Corsica. Eighty percent of the French people live in urban areas. The population density is 259 people per sq. mi. (100 people per km^2). (All figures based on 1988 census.)

Cities:	1982 Census	1989 Estimate
Paris	2,176,243	2,188,918
Marseille	874,436	878,689
Lyon	413,095	418,476
Toulouse	347,995	354,289
Nice	337,085	338,486
Strasbourg	248,712	252,264
Nantes	240,539	247,227
Bordeaux	208,159	211,197
St. Étienne	208,159	not available
Le Havre	199,388	not available

Occupations: Services, 64 percent; industry, 32 percent; agriculture, 4 percent.

GEOGRAPHY

Land Regions: There are ten principal land regions in France: (1) Brittany-Normandy Hills, (2) Northern France Plains, (3) Northeastern Plateaus, (4) Rhine Valley, (5) Aquitanian Lowlands, (6) Central Highlands, (7) French Alps and Jura Mountains, (8) Mediterranean Lowlands and Rhône-Saône Valley, (9) Pyrenees Mountains, and (10) the island of Corsica.

Borders: Italy, Spain, Switzerland, West Germany, Belgium, and Luxembourg

Highest Point: Mont Blanc, 15,771 ft. (4,807 m)

Lowest Point: Below sea level along delta of the Rhône River

Coastline: 2,300 mi. (3,701 km)

Greatest Distances: North to south—590 mi. (950 km)
East to west—605 mi. (974 km)

Area: Metropolitan France and Corsica, 211,208 sq. mi. (547,026 km²)

Rivers: The Rhine, forming part of France's boundary with Germany, is the main inland waterway in Europe. The Loire, about 650 miles (1,050 km) long, is the longest river entirely within France. Other major rivers include the Somme, Seine, Saône, Rhône, Marne, and Aisne.

Mountains: The Pyrenees Mountains extend between France and Spain and rise from 8,000 to 10,000 ft. (2,438 to 3,048 m). The French Alps between France, Italy, and Switzerland, the country's highest mountains, include Mont Blanc which soars to 15,771 ft. (4,807 m). Massif Central, a rugged plateau, covers one-sixth of the whole area of France and rises to about 6,000 ft. (1,829 m). The Jura Mountains, between France and Germany, are much lower at 5,653 ft. (1,723 m).

Climate: France's climate is quite varied. The differences in climate depend on the distance from the Atlantic Ocean or the Mediterranean Sea and the elevation above sea level. The west coast along the Atlantic experiences a rainy climate, with mild winters and cool summers. Inland areas have mild summers and cold winters in the north and hot summers and mild winters in the south, with medium rainfall year round. The mountainous areas receive the most precipitation (rain, snow, and other forms of moisture). Heavy snows fall in the Alps and Jura Mountains, and there are permanent glaciers in the Alps. The Mediterranean lowlands have hot, dry summers and mild winters.

Forests: About a fifth of France is covered with forests. Varieties of trees include pine, cork oak, ash, beech, cypress, and olive.

Minerals: Iron ore is the most important mineral. Also found in France are deposits of bauxite (to make aluminum), potash, copper, lead, uranium, and zinc. Important coal deposits are found in northern and central France, and some natural gas, petroleum, and salt deposits also exist.

ECONOMY AND INDUSTRY

Principal Products
Agriculture: Wheat is France's leading crop. Other important crops include chicory, colza, flax, flowers, fruits, hops, rice, rye, sugar beets, and tobacco. Beef and dairy cattle, sheep, hogs, goats, and chickens are also raised. Grapes, grown throughout France except in the far north, are used to make wine.

Mining: Iron ore, bauxite, coal, gypsum, potash, lead, zinc, copper, and uranium are mined in France.

Manufacturing: The manufacturing of automobiles and aircraft is very important to France. Also produced are iron, steel, aluminum, chemicals, furniture, and electrical and nonelectrical machinery. Other industries include jewelry, leather products, paper, perfume, textiles, cheese, and wine.

Electrical Power: Nuclear power provides 65 percent of the electrical power. The remainder of the electricity comes from coal-burning plants as well as hydroelectric and tidal power plants.

Fishing: The principal commercial fish are cod, mackerel, mussels, oysters, pollack, sardines, tuna, and whiting, producing a yearly catch of 807,000 short tons (732,000 metric tons).

Communication: About 120 daily newspapers are published in France, with a circulation of more than 10 million copies. The government owns one radio network and three television networks; it also oversees France's motion picture industry. Telegraph and telephone lines reach all parts of the country.

Transportation: France's government-owned railroad system has about 22,000 mi. (35,000 km) of track. There are about 50,500 mi. (81,270 km) of national highways and 263,500 mi. (424,060 km) of local roads. There are about 19 million cars in France, about one for every third person. Over 10,000 ships and barges navigate France's 4,780 mi. (7,693 km) of interconnecting navigable rivers and canals. Orly Airport near Paris, the busiest in France, serves about 17 million passengers a year. Charles de Gaulle Airport also serves Paris. Air France, jointly owned by the government and private investors, travels to seventy-five countries. A government-owned airline, Air Inter, travels among large French cities.

EVERYDAY LIFE

Food: Cooking is treated as an art in France. Many regions, cities, and restaurants have their own specialties, such as truffles in the Guyenne region, snails in Burgundy, sausages in Arles and Lyon, omelets in Mont St. Michel, and pressed duck in Paris. Unless one is entertaining, though, the everyday fare is simple. The typical breakfast consists of bread, butter, and jam with croissants on Sunday. Lunch is the big meal and usually includes several courses: meat, vegetables, fruit, and dessert. Dinner, eaten around 7:30 P.M., may include soup, salad, quiche lorraine or cold meat, cheese, and fruit. Wine is drunk quite often at meals; children are occasionally allowed a taste. The per capita consumption of wine is high.

Holidays: Many holidays in France celebrate major religious events in the Roman Catholic church. They include Shrove Tuesday, the last day before Lent, celebrated with a carnival called Mardi Gras. French children receive gifts on Noël

(Christmas) and chocolate eggs and chickens on Pâques (Easter). Gifts are also given on Le Jour de l'An (New Year's Day). Church bells are never rung from Good Friday to Easter. The French national holiday, Bastille Day, July 14, is celebrated by parades and fireworks. On May 1, friends and relatives give one another lilies of the valley. This is supposed to bring good luck and happiness. Most villages honor their local patron saint with a festival in July.

Sports: The most popular sports event in France is the "Tour de France," a several-week-long bicycle race. More than one hundred professional cyclists race across the countryside. Soccer is the most popular team sport. The French also play "boules," a bowling game played outdoors with metal balls. Tennis, hiking, camping, bicycling, fishing, skiing, rugby, and swimming are also popular.

Schools: The school year begins in mid-September with seventy-four vacation days in the summer, fifteen in the spring, and thirteen during winter. Children attend school Saturday mornings, but have Wednesdays free to attend cultural events. Education is free and controlled by the Ministry of National Education. Children between the ages of six and sixteen must attend school. Nursery schools are available at government expense for children ages two to six. Students from six to thirteen attend elementary schools, most of which are separate for boys and girls. After this, they attend a general high school or a trade school. The general high schools (called *colleges* or *lycées*) prepare students to enter universities. The baccalaureate examination after high school is so difficult that up to 50 percent of the students fail. Vocational (trade) schools last three to five years and include job training. No tuition is charged for the universities. There are more than sixty small state universities. Because of the reforms made after the student uprisings in 1968, students at each university choose their own courses and teaching methods. Students also take part in university administration.

Culture: France has about thirty government-owned museums. The best known is the Louvre in Paris, one of the world's largest art museums. There are seventy-five legitimate theatres in Paris alone offering the broadest range of productions, as well as numerous nightclubs and music halls. Comédie Français and Théâtre de France are the two fine national theatres. Paris is one of the best-known cities for contemporary music, and its opera house is the largest theater in the world. Public libraries are found in all large cities. The national library, the Bibliothèque Nationale in Paris, is one of the largest libraries in western Europe.

IMPORTANT DATES

600 B.C. — Marseille founded by Greeks

500 B.C. — Celts invade Gaul

390 B.C. — Gauls sack Rome, first of many conflicts

59-52 B.C. — Caesar conquers Gaul

257 — Invasion of Franks and Alamanni

541 — Gallo-Romans defeat Attila's Huns

496 — Conversion of Clovis I to Christianity

507 — Clovis defeats Visigoths

732 — King Charles Martel checks Arabs at Poitiers

800 — Charlemagne becomes Holy Roman Emperor

911 — Duchy of Normandy founded

1066 — William of Normandy invades England, defeats Harold at the Battle of Hastings

1095 — Crusades launched at Clermont

1099 — Capture of Jerusalem by Crusaders

late 1100s — Cathedrals of Chartres and Notre Dame begun

1152 — France loses Aquitaine to England

1204 — England loses Normandy, Anjou, and other territories

1223 — Louis VIII conquers the south of France

1309-78 — The popes live in Avignon

1337-1453 — Hundred Years' War

1347 — Black Death, a terrible plague, strikes Europe

1356 — The English advance; King John defeated by the Black Prince at Poitiers

1429 — Joan of Arc raises siege of Orleans

1431 — Joan of Arc burned at stake in Rouen

1453 — End of Hundred Years' War with English retreat to Calais

1517 — Luther publishes Wittenburg Protest; Protestant Reformation begins

1519 — A Hapsburg (Charles I of Spain) elected Holy Roman Emperor (as Charles V), beginning Franco-German rivalry

1533 — Calvin reverts to Protestantism

1547 — Mary, Queen of Scots, taken to France; Henry marries Catherine de Medicis

1562-98 — Religious wars: Catholics versus Huguenots

1594 — Henry IV renounces Protestant faith, becomes a Catholic

1598 — Edict of Nantes: Huguenots tolerated, freedom of worship allowed

1608 — Champlain founds Quebec

1618-48 — Thirty Years' War

1685 — The Edict of Nantes revoked, causing emigration of Huguenots

1689-98 — King William's War; France defeated

1702-13 — Queen Anne's War; France hands over Newfoundland, Nova Scotia, and Gibraltar to England

1744-48 — King George's War; France defeated

1754-63 — French and Indian Wars; France gives up Canada and all possessions east of Mississippi to England

1756-63 — Seven Years' War

1778-83 — French assist American revolutionaries

1789-92 — French Revolution begins with calling of Estates General, ends with founding of a republic; Bastille captured on July 14, 1789

1792-95 — The Convention in control; Reign of Terror begins

1792-1804 — First Republic; Girondists declare war on Prussia and Austria

1794 — Admiral Nelson of England destroys French fleet

1795-99 — Convention dissolved; Directory begins; Napoleon Bonaparte is its champion

1798 — Battle of the Nile

1799-1804 — The Consulate begins, with Napoleon as First Consul

1805 — French defeated by Nelson at Battle of Trafalgar; Russia and Austria beaten at Austerlitz

1805-12 — Napoleon conquers large part of Europe, is defeated in Russia

1814 — Napoleon exiled to island of Elba

1815 — Return of Napoleon for one hundred days; defeated at Waterloo; abdicated again

1830 — July revolution deposes Charles X

1846-47—Severe industrial and agricultural depression

1848—Louis Philippe deposed; Louis Napoléon, nephew of Bonaparte, elected president

1848-52—Second Republic

1870—Franco-Prussian War; Flaubert and Baudelaire writing

1870-1944—Third Republic; sixteen presidents in seventy-five years

1871—Alsace-Lorraine ceded to Germany

1914-18—First World War; France fights on Allied side

1939-40—World War II; France on Allied side

1940-42—Germany occupies northern France

1942—The Japanese capture the French colonies of Indochina

1942-44—The Germans occupy all of France

1944—Allied D-Day invasion of Normandy on June 4

1946-54—Indochinese War; trouble in Africa; independence for Morocco and Tunisia

1947—Fourth Republic established

1949—France joins with fourteen other Western nations to form the North Atlantic Treaty Organization (NATO)

1954—Vietnam gains independence; revolution breaks out in Algeria

1958—France joins European Economic Community (EEC); De Gaulle elected president, proposes new constitution with presidential form of government; Fifth Republic begins

1960—France explodes its first atomic bomb

1962—France grants independence to Algeria; new constitution approved

1967—France leaves NATO

1968—Widespread disruption initiated by student uprisings in Paris brings country to a standstill; De Gaulle promises reform, asserts authority

1969—De Gaulle resigns as president, succeeded by Georges Pompidou

1974—Pompidou dies and is succeeded by Valéry Giscard d'Estaing

1981—François Mitterrand leads Socialist party to victory; the centralized prefectural system instituted by Napoleon in 1793 is dismantled, turning significant local decision-making over to town and regional councils

1986—Coalition candidates led by Jacques Chirac win a slim majority in legislative elections and begin challenging socialist policies of François Mitterrand

1988—Francois Mitterand re-elected to second seven-year term

1989—Nationwide celebration begins of the 200th anniversary of the French Revolution

1990—Violent storms with winds over 100 miles an hour claim 8 lives in France

IMPORTANT PEOPLE

André Marie Ampère (1775-1836), physicist and mathematician known for his contributions to the study of electrodynamics and his studies of the relationship between electricity and magnetism; the ampere, the basic unit of electrical current, is named for him

Simone de Beauvoir (1912-86), writer and disciple of existentialist Jean-Paul Sartre; a teacher before the war, she became famous for her brilliant postwar novels *Men Are All Mortal* and *The Mandarins*

Albert Camus (1913-60), journalist, essayist, novelist, and playwright associated with the existentialist movement

Paul Cézanne (1839-1906), painter; after studying with Pisarro, he developed a postimpressionist style notable for its accentuation of geometric forms and slight distortions that emphasize the solidity of objects

Marie Sklodowski Curie (1867-1934), Polish-French physicist born in Warsaw; together with husband Pierre, investigated the radioactivity of uranium and discovered two new elements; they shared the 1903 Nobel Prize in physics; Marie received the 1911 Nobel Prize in chemistry

Claude Debussy (1862-1918), an important composer, his revolutionary treatment of musical form and harmony helped change the direction of music in the 1900s

Edgar Degas (1834-1917), impressionist painter, he emphasized composition drawing and form more than light and color

Charles de Gaulle (1890-1970), outstanding French patriot, soldier, and statesman of the 1900s; led French resistance against Germany in World War II, and restored order in France after the war; guided formation of France's Fifth Republic in 1958, and served as its president until his resignation in 1969

Denis Diderot (1713-84), principal author of the famous *Encyclopédie*, in twenty-eight volumes, over which he labored for more than twenty years, assisted by Voltaire, Montesquieu, Rosseau, Buffon, and Jean d'Alembert

Paul Gauguin (1848-1903), postimpressionist painter whose work is noted for its massive simplified forms, impassive figures, and exotic backgrounds

Valéry Giscard d'Estaing (b. 1926), president of France 1974-81; founded the Independent Republican Party in 1962

Jean-Luc Godard (b. 1930), semisurrealist director-writer of the "New-Wave" cinema

Victor Marie Hugo (1802-85), poet and dramatist, his most famous novels are *The Hunchback of Notre-Dame* and *Les Misérables*

Antoine Laurent Lavoisier (1743-94), one of the founders of modern chemistry and one of the originators of the modern system of chemical nomenclature; guillotined during the French Revolution

Louis Malle (b. 1932), "New-Wave" director of *Pretty Baby* and *My Dinner with André,* and other films

Olivier Messiaen (b. 1908), composer known for using unusual musical ideas in his compositions

François Maurice Mitterrand (b. 1916), elected president of France in 1981; leader of Socialist party and the country's first leftist president since 1958

Louis Pasteur (1822-95), chemist and microbiologist, inventor of the process of pasteurization

Henri Philippe Pétain (1856-1951), national hero of France because of his military leadership in World War I; later tried for treason for his collaboration with the Germans in World War II; convicted and died in prison at age ninety-five

Georges Jean Raymond Pompidou (1911-74), president of France 1969-74; member of the Union of Democrats for the Republic, a political party that supported de Gaulle

George Sand (Amandine Aurore Lucie Dupin Dudevant) (1804-76), early feminist, socialist, humanitarian, and apostle of free love; more famous for her lovers and friends than for her novels

Jean-Paul Sartre (1905-80), playwright, novelist, and philosopher known as the postwar prophet of existentialism

Henri de Toulouse-Lautrec (1864-1901), painter and poster designer of noble lineage; as famous for his physical deformity, alcoholism, and sordid associations as for his postimpressionist paintings

François Truffaut (1932-84), "New-Wave" director and critic, whose films include *Jules and Jim* and *The 400 Blows*

Jules Verne (1828-1905), author and novelist who wrote some of the first science fiction stories; he forecast the invention of the airplane, submarine, television, guided missile, and space satellite

François Marie Arouet Voltaire (1694-1778), author of *Candide;* an assimilator of ideas rather than an original thinker, he believed literature should be useful; best known for his attacks on the church and for his defense of John Locke's liberal political views

Émile Zola (1840-1902), novelist born in Paris; an uncompromising naturalist, he portrayed all humans as helpless victims of heredity and environment

INDEX

Page numbers that appear in boldface type indicate illustrations

About the Authors

Peter Moss lives in the countryside of Sussex, England. A writer and former teacher, he has authored over forty books, many of them for English schoolchildren. He often vacations in France, where he stays in a chateau enjoying French hospitality as well as the superb food and wine.

Thelma Palmer, also a writer and former teacher, lives on a small, isolated island in the Pacific Northwest. She believes that travel is a wonderful way to learn and teach, and for many summers she has traveled in Europe with students. It was on these trips that she came to love the history, culture, and people of France.